1/0 ⌐

NEW STORIES 7

New Stories 7

Edited by Alan Ross

Hutchinson
London Melbourne Sydney Auckland Johannesburg
**in association with The Arts Council
of Great Britain and PEN**

Hutchinson & Co. (Publishers) Ltd

An imprint of the Hutchinson Publishing Group

17–21 Conway Street, London W1P 6JD

Hutchinson Group (Australia) Pty Ltd
30–32 Cremorne Street, Richmond South, Victoria 3121
PO Box 151, Broadway, New South Wales 2007

Hutchinson Group (NZ) Ltd
32–34 View Road, PO Box 40–086, Glenfield, Auckland 10

Hutchinson Group (SA) (Pty) Ltd
PO Box 337, Bergvlei 2012, South Africa

First published 1982

Set in VIP Bembo by D. P. Media Limited, Hitchin, Hertfordshire

Printed in Great Britain by The Anchor Press Ltd and bound by Wm
Brendon & Son Ltd, both of Tiptree, Essex

British Library Cataloguing in Publication Data

New stories.
7
1. Short stories, English
I. Alan Ross
823'.01'08[FS]   PR1309.S5

ISBN 0 09 147930 4

The Arts Council of Great Britain and PEN at regular intervals
invite writers to send in short stories and poems for consideration for
publication in their series of anthologies. Information appears in the
national press, and further details can be obtained from the secretary,
PEN, 7 Dilke Street, London SW3 4JE.

Contents

P. J. Riordan   **Gently Down the Stream**   7
Graham Swift   **Hide and Seek**   29
Peter Parker   **Late Flowering**   46
John Haylock   **Setting the World Aright**   61
Julian Barnes   **One of a Kind**   74
Nancy Oliver   **The Outsider**   82
James Thurlby   **Hidden Agenda**   95
Anne Aylor   **No Angel Hotel**   108
Colin Beadon   **And Roses**   114
A. R. Barton   **Going Places**   121
Anne Spillard   **Two Heads**   130
John Rudge   **For the Sake of the School**   148
Morris Lurie   **Swallows**   153
Alison Brackenbury   **Winter**   167
Glyn Hughes   **The Human Sacrifice**   179
Marshall Walker   **Five and Twenty Ponies**   190
Alan Seymour   **The Drowning**   199

Notes on the Authors   219

Gently Down the Stream
P. J. Riordan

Viewed from the other side of the stream, I must appear as a participant in a tableau representing paradise. It is mid-morning, in the middle of a particularly hot summer and I am sitting in a canvas chair, sipping chilled martini and lemon, in the shade of an apple tree, a library book in my lap. That the garden seat is not specifically designed for comfort and that the book, with its British Safety Standard seal of approval, is by Hemingway are facts not distantly apparent. Small trout are developing into worthwhile trout in the stream that meets and makes the bottom border of our garden and as the passersby linger to count fish, their eyes elevate enviously to check the property value. I like to watch those aspiring eyes. I cannot afford to pity the working class few, who find time between overtime and the squalor of their cityscape, from whence I fortunately emerged, to loiter by my house and betray their ambitions to the most anonymous of strangers. The rates alone on their dream are unforgivably high. I have the fishing rights to this part of the river, but no tackle and no interest in fishing.

My wife is polishing the dining room parquet-tiled floor. She is wearing white shorts, a navy tee-shirt and white plimsolls with yellow ankle socks. Through the open french windows I can see only her white shorts, creasing and straightening in the dark interior. The floor polisher whirls wax silently indoors, while over my head, in the neat azure, a helicopter patrols the watermeadows and lower city slopes as part of the most recent external security measures for the city's top security and terrorist institution. As the helicopter fades across the valley the breeze carries the lively beat of an army band practising on the barrack square. Between duties the city streets were a pot-pourri of uniforms and regimentation.

A young man, back bowed in heavy duty working clothes, follows the path along the river. He is wearing a dusty brown cap, but his coat, his only acknowledgment to the heat, is slung across his shoulder. His index finger hooks through the tiny loop on the inside of the jacket's collar. Focusing on his weary wending figure, over my reading glasses, I am sure I know this man. He drags his feet past the bottom of the garden, kicking small cyclones of dust. His eyes penetrate my presence, he stares at the house. I stand clutching Hemingway to my knees and my wife stops polishing to conspicuously close the french windows. She waves her fingers nervously and I am able to smile.

Later, over the burnt top half of a toasted teacake, my curiosity is satisfied. I recall that in those gloomy days of employment, before I was given the chance of voluntary redundancy, I used to share a locker in the rest room with that young man. We were buddies and workmates. I was a stoker at the city council rubbish dump and waterworks and he was the vermin controller at the nearby and associate sewage farm. Our lunch hours more or less coincided, although he had to cycle one flat mile to the rest room, a handbasin and his sandwiches. Why we should choose to congregate in this ramshackle cabin, unsuitable even for livestock, is an enigma. A roof, cobwebbed corners, two chairs, a bench, a pile of mildewed magazines, a tabletop ringed with stains, a window of sanded glass, or of clear glass with dust so permanently adhered to its surface as to appear sanded. Daylight scarcely bothered to penetrate this north-facing opening, in winter the wind was hardly checked. A crisp rag curtain soaked up careless, early morning seepage of natural light and overnight condensation, until the first bleary-eyed employee to hang his coat switched on the twin bulbs, lit the paraffin stove and effectively abolished the necessity for sunlight within the cramped spaces of our sanctuary. He washed his hands in the enamel-crazed handbasin and dried them in front of the paraffin burner rather than risk soiling them on the grubby towel provided, once upon a time, by the management. He was by no means a hygiene fanatic, although the senior stokers scoffed at him, called him 'pansy', and deliberately defiled their huge stokers' shovelling hands.

I am trying to remember his name.

He tolerated their barbed fun and malicious games, born of resentments and jealousies like a saint, a martyr, for I too felt the pricks of their spite, but was never called into the direct line of vicious fire. Their persistent malevolence should have told us we were like landed fish. Fortunately I was thrown back, he, so it would appear, has stubbornly and singularly withstood the pressures of their childish heckling alone.

He wheels his bicycle through the water-meadows, along the potholed public footpath, that follow the stream that flows at the bottom of my garden, to his rooms in a terrace in the lower city suburbs.

My wife of white shorts and white plimsolls is the catalyst in my good fortune. She has always favoured white, since our registry office wedding. Turning to the house, I drop Hemingway, page uppermost on my chair, and the pages unread turn in the bright, light breeze. I can never concentrate enough to read in the open air, even when the book is not my wife's third or fourth choice from the library. She has three tickets too many, but flatters herself to deceive the librarian with whom we occasionally mix socially. To her credit, the librarian never discusses the odd reading habits of her general public. The most popular topic of conversation, measured in words, gas expended and alcohol consumed, is painting, of which everyone says they have and know their preference, in which my wife has a neglected talent and about which I am completely ignorant.

I cannot see my wife, although I shade my eyes to the reflections at each ground floor window. She refuses to burn electricity for light until early evening, being bad for the eyesight and an extravagance of the lower classes, whose windows are generally smaller and directed across the line of the sun's ascendence and descendence. Unadulterated snobbery, as the windows of her house are described as quaintly small. A rush of water flushed down the outside fall-pipe from the upstairs bathroom. I return to the garden chair, close Hemingway, close my eyes and close my thighs on my closed palms.

The helicopter is sweeping with remarkable alacrity at an alarmingly low altitude. My wife makes telephone calls, which she claims are heeded, but I recognize the ill will in this generous regard for our security. I keep my eyes closed to hide any fear, any guilt.

My friend the vermin controller, whatever his elusive name, has not talked to me, nor acknowledged my existence for years, although he passes my house and garden twice every day. The prelude to this marathon silence was a trivial incident, as is often the case. His trappist stamina came from injured pride. Shortly after my wedding, a spontaneous private affair, he was cycling along the footpath in the face of an ancient by-law and without clips, when he was taken aback to find me so easily ensconsed in the 'young widow's' garden. My new wife had been a regular focus of speculative gossip in the rest room at work and in the public house afterwards. When I, still suffering the blissful after-effects of a dazzling Caribbean honeymoon, was preparing to launch myself into a cross-channel discussion, announcing my acceptance of certain vows, my wife, exercising her marital privilege, appeared from nowhere to rescue me from a near suicidal social gaffe. Later, it was explained, over pre-dinner tipple that certain occupations, thus certain of my old acquaintances, were not socially elect. To her credit, my wife was a patient, if persistent tutor.

I open my eyes to the white scent of her presence and must confess to letting the perfume carry me into unspecified fantasies. She had washed her hair and wrapped a white towel loosely around her head. When I look up, she is silently angling an empty tumbler in front of my face demanding a cocktail. She contorts her face, expressing extreme displeasure at the absence of ice. She is without doubt a beautiful, white woman, her brown complexion and white accessories politely concealing her age. I go to the refrigerator for more ice and through word association from brand names of freezers to surnames I recall the rat controller's christian name. Martin. He does his job well, there are no rodents in our garden.

The story we wrote for my wife over meat-pie suppers and pints of best bitter was grossly inaccurate. We called her 'widow', when in fact the man with whom she cohabited had recently left her for reasons of emotional stress, dismay and disaffection. This, the cottage and contents she fictitiöusly inherited, was in reality a property of the public school, leased to that infamously anonymous 'respectable couple'. After my predecessor's inconvenient departure, she remained an illegal tenant for only a short period, until our impetuous marriage.

When I return, ice melting on a tablespoon, she has finished the drink and persuaded her Siamese cat to lick the empty jug. I walk slowly to the bottom of the garden, deliberately show-ing my disgust and plop the ice into the warm river. I did not expect the cubes to resurface and bob gently down the stream. I watch them for a moment then redirect my attention to the mooring post, where my rowing boat had been secured. A piece of rope pulls downstream. The attachment, an unfash-ionable craft painted municipal green, had been cut from its moorings three nights ago. I found the wreckage the next morning about a mile downstream. My wife offered me a sympathetic snap of Kit-Kat, when I betrayed the wreck was beyond salvage. I had vague notions of hiring out the boat on a daily rate during the school holidays, but my wife abhorred the idea and fought my proposals vigorously, threatening to make matchsticks out of the boat if my demeaning business intentions floated. The occasion never arose, my boat and its history broke up a mile downstream, abruptly terminating the felons' joy-ride afloat.

I have been putting down poison for the cat, obviously in insufficient quantities as the beast still disturbs the peace with a wretched cry and my peace of mind with its suspicious squint.

I have been tempted to abandon the snoozing bundle of pussy in a carrier bag, on the doorstep of a Chinese takeaway, but she sleeps with one eye open and I have no real desire to return to the dim lights of the lower city.

I clipped across the fractured tarmac in a hurry, skipping potholes and horse droppings alike. The metal segments on my hobnails echoed through these early morning empty streets. I noticed I had left the light on in my attic room, the one light in the terrace at this ungodly hour and although the yellow bulb would burn over my Baby Belling throughout the day and waste the metered electricity I decided not to return. I was already late for work. I pulled my grey cap down over my brow and turned the corner into a busier thoroughfare where only a third of the streetlights were now working. I had been informed by duplicated news-sheet, folded through the letterbox, that there was no money in the civic coffers to pay the exhorbitant wages and no economic brains to enforce the complicated productivity schemes demanded by maintenance crews. By similar methods of propaganda the trade unions involved requested the concerned brethren to appreciate that their members should not have to reduce their living standards for the benefit of the community's standard of living.

As I crossed the main street, a public service vehicle was leaving the depot, overtaking two broken-down, cheap, imported cars, abandoned and stripped where they had stalled. Other buses with blackened interiors waited in queues for their daily schedules to commence. A silver Mercedes with tinted windows and an abusive horn reminded the few sleepy pedestrians of their lack of wealth and their inextricable circumstance.

For the final leg of my journey to work I turned towards the river, where I untied my rowing boat and pushed it out into midstream where the flow was stronger. The sound of the oars slicing the surface and the gentle undulations of water smacking the banks were my chronometer before daylight. I pulled the boat towards new grey sky and watched silhouettes of buildings and trees left behind. In winter I rowed the course by instinct, wrapped against the cold and damp, the elbows of my shirts all ripped or reinforced, by or for the rowing effort.

One of these shirts is now my gardening shirt and the others committed, at her suggestion, to refuse collection alongside several of her own pre-marital ensembles and her battered, fur, courting coat in which I found her irresistible.

Those bleak days of full time employment were not all bad. We made the most of our free time, with traditional lower-class gusto. Sitting in the Cricketers public bar, near the gentleman's run out late one Saturday morning, tapping my feet on the cracked linoleum, wiping the condensation from the outside of my straight pint glass, checking for sediment, flicking the corners of a deck of playing cards, I was waiting for Martin to make a hand at cribbage. I borrowed a damp cloth from the bar to wipe over the solid, laminated tabletop. The brittle surface layer had been picked from the corners by nervous fingernails. Dull grey smears replaced the rings of beer on the tabletop, dried copper overnight. Martin was taking his time shaving, polishing his spectacles, cleaning the spots off his mirror wondering whether to leave a negative area in which a moustache might grow. I had moved in recently to share-rent a small pre-second-world-war semi and to part ignore the garden behind, beyond kicking a plastic ball between upright garden replicas, from one patch of weeds to another. Through neglect, a vast privet hedge had monopolized the front garden. Here, privacy was the reward for idleness.

The landlady, in a vivid pink, two-piece suit and a blue-black, lacquered wig, moaned across the bar about the drastic effects of the previous night's overindulgence. Her femininity, like her virginity and lemonade bottles, was non returnable. She was under the doctor and, unfortunately, considering her vocation, an alcoholic since her husband's massive and fatal coronary. The brewery, although sympathetic, were putting the ravaged widow under considerable additional pressure to sell up and install herself in a sanitorium on the proceeds. She claimed their offers were more than generous, but women of all generations are notoriously stubborn, for which we must thank, or blame the suffragettes.

I bought another drink and passed the time of day with the cellarman. The landlady was standing by the cash register, staring vacantly at the queen's portrait on an old pound note, as if for inspiration, meanwhile the customer waiting impatiently for his change, snapped his fingers and returned her to her senses. She apologized, once again recounting the acid memories of her nocturnal movements.

Saturday dinner times were important sessions in Martin's religion, a ritual cleansing for the Saturday night self-sacrifice.

The helicopter swirling above returns me to this side of the fence with no ball in sight, nor weed to flatten. I join the cat in a weary sigh. Tired of the sun, she has found cool soil. I sprawl by her side and peevishly throw pebbles and blades of grass onto her bloated belly, to watch the fur shimmer and shiver. I would bury her here and now without resistance, but for the re-appearance of my wife, who attracts my attention by viciously planting a plimsoll in my kidneys. I roll and the cat bolts. There is a piece of liver in the refrigerator which I intend to lace and carelessly let slip in her path.

We attempt to eat lunch in silence, soup and a bread roll. My wife has the awful facility to scold me with her presence. The significant use of her napkin and the stern angle of her head are, at mealtimes, too well practised.

'I'm going out tonight,' she burns. 'I might be late.'

'The dramatic society or yoga?' I query sarcastically, sucking a crust of saturated Hovis as she scolds my tongue with her stare. I suppress further observations with soup. She curses every mouthful that might give me strength and I am truly mortified by each drop and nervous dribble of soup solid.

Over the years this classical dining room with its highly polished mahogany circular table, the glass-fronted china cabinet and set of high-backed chairs had taken on the dimensions of a torture chamber and the furniture its precise accoutrements. Static oil landscapes dominate the room. Whatever emotion or romantic feeling is present in their time-yellowed surfaces is lost by tasteful positioning on the Sanderson Regency stripes. As their overembellished gold-painted frames catch the corner of one uncritical eye they take on a false value. By accident or by design, I have never found myself standing directly in front of these evasive masterpieces. I cannot say with assurance if they are inhabited. I have never counted the spaces these artifacts harmoniously disguise, although in my mind's eye they are abundant, economically miniaturized to enhance the most awkward niche. I sense a grieving silence from the kitchen, a very feminine absence of noise and movement pushes me outside. I leave the french windows ajar and a light breeze lifts the olive-green curtains. Thin clouds are stretching across the blue, the weather is changing. An evening storm is forecast. My wife is going out at 7.30 to an action committee meeting and she will be spitefully late. She thinks I am having an affair with a girl I met last Thursday lunchtime when my wife was doing the rounds of the library, the building society and the more exclusive boutiques by taxi. I can feel a smear of soup hardening in the corner of my mouth. The view across the watermeadows, towards the motorway and Catherine's hill beyond, is magnificent. The motorway has removed the heavy traffic from congestion within the city walls, but in its wake has also brought hundreds of middle-aged, middle-minded liberals violently protesting about the wilful erosion of the landscape. Now the battlers have left, their minds scarred by weals of tarmac, to rewrite their placards and sharpen their resolve and the motorway has sunk into picturesque obscurity behind a sheltering line of trees. Occasionally a ten-second buzz of activity would drift from that direction, but, in general, the professional landscapers have done a marvellous job.

My wife's vision has been permanently impaired by her bitter defeat. She cried as the wounds left by the mechanical excavators healed. I foolishly tried to comfort her, pointing to greater follies, such as being on the flight path of supersonic civil aircraft, and the helicopter patrols. However, my comforter's hands were spiked with the knowledge that these were two other of her failed campaigns. I talked to her of progress, a word omitted from the liberals' vocabulary, on whose faces a puzzled look appears to shade their understanding and colour their interpretation of the word, where such plans threaten property values and open spaces. She cried at the idea of progress like a baby will cry at the mention of the word 'monster'. Before we were married, these rolling tufts and turves, copses and meandering tributaries, an area of outstanding natural beauty considered dangerous for children below the age of consent, were our courting grounds. In the daytime we shared our walks with assorted couples of similar intent. All ages below pensionable age walked hand in hand, only the arthritic and immobile being wheeled to a carpark with a panoramic view. Long after sunset our passions were undivided and in the privacy of the moonlight the seduction occurred.

To a vehement anti–progressive I must have appeared an eccentric figure rowing to and from work and although appearances are deceptive I was momentarily unbalanced in falling for her triple assault. On that long-remembered, long-regretted day, I finished work early and, being in no particular hurry, I tied up to watch the final overs of the public school's first activities of the summer. I was not aware of any scoreboard. Even after the last ball was bowled and the fielding captain sauntered over to the surviving batsmen, I was not certain from the sporting exchange of expressions who had emerged victorious. With the precociousness of a prospective head boy, he shook hands with the umpires and collected the stumps. The pace was gentle and undemanding, the only sign of exasperation coming as the batsmen left the field. Following a word with his lounging colleagues, a bat was unceremoniously discarded by one of them. The culprit was immediately expelled from the company to begin arduous circuits of the boundary as punishment for his lapse of sports-manship. His team-mates left him lapping the playing field as he chased the secret number of his repentance. He was not overjoyed at seeing me, with my distinct lack of pedigree, lazing in the cool shade of the horse-chestnut trees, but I remained to cultivate his contempt. For the first time I was able to understand the fascination of public executions. I was chilled and a little damp by the time I granted him a reprieve, for apart from admiring his honesty in adhering to his punishment until dusk, I could not help wondering what worse thing he was avoiding. In the distance a regimental band was practising marches, traditional and coarse arrangements of popular modern classics, clashes of culture never entirely satisfactory. Clashes of cymbals out of time. By the river, with a slight mist lifting off the watercourse, the darkness was more intense and hastened my efforts to depart. I untied the boat and began to row hard against the clock and the current, with every intention of meeting Martin in the Cricketers for supper, a regular rendezvous, all circumstances permitting. I made heavy, but steady headway and had been rowing for no more than ten minutes when her initial assault was launched. The anonymity of the attack was the most terrifying part of it. As I was passing beneath a low pedestrian bridge, an uncomfortable manoeuvre at any time, a weighty object entered the water close enough to my bows to cause the displaced water to flood my boat. The prime, most obvious culprit was the irked public schoolboy, the miffed jogger. The muffled giggle that followed the attack strengthened my views. Despite my vulnerability I hailed my assailant with such ferocity as to cause a gender change, for from the shadows of the footbridge a girl in flimsy white dance-darted. Freed from height restrictions, I was now able to stand in my unstable boat. My heart beating dangerously, I drifted back on the current and clouted my head on a plywood sign reading 'Private Footbridge. Property the Public School'. When I was able to return to more peaceful striking, my imagination was stoked with thoughts of relating an ornamental version of this story to Martin, the normally accepted and celebrated tall-story-teller in our group. However, the second phase of the attack came less than a hundred yards upstream. But whereas the essence of the preceding assault was surprise, I had forewarning of this follow-up strike. Turning at the waist to re-establish the desired direction I chanced to glimpse a swift silhouette dodging between startled ducks and shrubbery, too close for me to concentrate my body to a more determined posture of self-defence, but far enough away to alter my position in the universe. I wheeled skilfully towards the opposite bank from my would-be assailant. As it came, the attack was verbal rather than physical and its manner taunting rather than aggressive. The tune was a monster in its simplicity, but the verse and chorus were more difficult to remember. Her intentions were so obviously naked, goose-pimples stood up on my arms. It is hard to imagine my wife playing such games; needless to say, they have not continued.

Our final encounter that evening was more conclusive and I was naive enough, perhaps optimistic enough, to believe that this scene was in progress or have my later loud embellishments in the Cricketers become confused with reality? Although I rowed ardently and time's flight has taken liberties with my fancies, I can distinctly recall the commotion as she tripped over her Siamese cat, my life's stumbling block and the most recent target for my revenge. For the first sight of my wife, I found her collapsed and groaning at the end of her garden, her flimsy white dress up round her head and her lower limbs revealingly displayed. When I arrived on the scene her bottom was rising like a moon over water. Her small white knickers have been rudely imprinted on my mind ever since. Gallantly, I carried her in through the french windows and looked around a severe English interior for any padded surface on which to settle her. On that night of nights, all I could find was a real goatskin rug, with authentic goat smells covering a section of highly polished parquet flooring. My inexperience left her in tears and her clothes in tatters. The cause of her tearful overflow was not recognition of my unbridled passion, but uncontrollable mirth as we flew across the slippery floor on a magic carpet ride. She limped to the bath-room and I chose this moment to leave discreetly. In the boat my arms were shaking with the effort of it all. Rushing to make my alibi in the Cricketers, my stroke was hasty and untidy, so I was saturated and limp as I tied up.

Eagerness to communicate with my fellows loosened my tongue and several pints of best bitter compounded rather than concealed my felony, if felony it was. I left the Cricketers a lion that night.

The helicopter circles to its right and from the city it dips and accelerates around the perimeter of the watermeadows, fol-lowing the carriageway along the base of Catherine's hill, until its circuit is complete. Then, once again tumbling to the right, it flaps out of sight beyond the viaduct and back across the city. From the ground, to this inexperienced observer, it appears the pilots are overextending their machines to combat the monotony of their mission. From the gound the clouds boiled to torment.

My wife has written a letter to the local newspaper this morning, after breakfast of half a grapefruit and black coffee, to be published notwithstanding misprints in next week's edition. A grave epistle concerning the rumoured military manoeuvres in her beloved meadows. Obviously in such an insecure location, no grand military secrets, nor valuable strategies would be revealed, but my wife is concerned lest the whole structure of civilization should crumble within the frame of our picture windows. I am more inclined to watch and wait. She illustrated her opinions in gentle watercolours, with Sunday mornings, churchbells, strolling parishioners, pensioners and lazy fishermen. But is her memory so short that she has forgotten the real hallowedness of this plot of land? In far off days of do and dare, we had frolicked there and once by the river we had flattened the reeds and made love. The thought of the army, with those privates' diving elbows and driving knees, exercising there in vital cowboy games without horses, without live bullets and without good-dead indians, was perverse to say the least. And if my objections are read as pure romanticism hers are selfish and equally false.

That she is having an affair I do not doubt. She is still an attractive woman and capable of infidelities. The hate dormant, deep in her warm brown eyes, awakes coldly in my presence and to watch this performance in company is to see light playing on a turning diamond. I had no proof, nor wanted any.

There is a piece of Paraquat pig's liver in the refrigerator; when my wife goes out this evening I will leave the tainted morsel where her curious Siamese will find it.

She finally uncurls her hair at half past four letting the thick white towel fall at her feet. She shakes her head. During the previous forty-five minutes she had peered closely into the full-length bedroom mirror, plucking her eyebrows with trembling tweezers, spitting fire and softening her skin in herbal creams. I enjoy watching her, thrilled by the intensity with which she approaches beauty and amazed by her stamina, standing now without complaint for over an hour. I was stretched out on her bed, with my fingers clasped behind my neck to lift my head. She was appalled by the untidiness of my habits, but I claimed a mild bout of sunstroke and was permitted to stay, although she hated my intrusion on her privacy. She tipped back her head slightly and brushed the full length of her hair. She had already changed out of her blue tee shirt into a white cotton shirt and now that too was removed. It is approaching five o'clock as she lets down her shorts and stands naked in front of her mirror, twisting her torso, playfully patting her taut stomach and lifting her bosom through nostalgia.

I hoist myself erect and watch as an avalanche of flesh rolls from my stomach and settles between my thighs. My wife looks across in disgust, before turning to find solace in music via her bedroom hi-fi and tonic water via a glass of gin. I lock myself in the upstairs bathroom.

It is dark inside the house as I flush the toilet and go down-stairs. She is looking at the whites of her eyes in a handmirror, but immediately stashes it in her handbag, frowning, when she sees me descending.

'I'm going soon,' she informs me politely. She looks anxious to impress in a long white dress I have not seen before. She is beautiful, she is hard. I cannot look at her, I cannot answer her. In the final analysis I am a jealous man and despise that passion in me. I cannot stand to feel my heartbeat.

The cat is darting around the dark room in an uncharacteristic display of paranoia, squealing and coughing in a frenzy. We heard the tyres of a car crushing gravel in our drive and without question or farewell I went into the kitchen to cook a solitary supper. It is 7.45 by the clock on the electric cooker. The pig's liver is missing from the refrigerator. I grill a block of frozen cod, neither nourishing nor appetising. My normal culinary enthusiasm is sadly lacking and the contents of the refrigerator, now the suspect has been scoffed, are uninspiring. I find my menu fillers in tins, without the need for cooking instructions. I eat as I cook and I save the labour of washing up by this economy.

The evil-smelling, green slurry I discover on my return to the dining room is the first indication of the cat's mortality and it would certainly have spoiled my appetite had I witnessed its occurrence. The limp corpse has settled heavily by the french windows, on its face a morbid revengeful grin. I put the cat in a cardboard box, cover it with newspaper and leave the makeshift coffin by the kitchen door for disposal tomorrow. My wife might insist on interment beneath the begonias. I preferred cremation and delivery to the council dustcart, but it is her decision. The smell from the motion on the wooden floor lingers unpleasantly even after I have deposited a stained newspaper parcel in the dustbin. The rain has begun, thunder crackles in the distance.

I spend the evening in the cold company of the black and white portable in the lounge, in summer a room rarely used. The sound is down, the programmes are standard for the hour. I drink several glasses of gin to ease the monotony, I grow full of self-pity and find it easier to present the blame at her door.

After her introductory offer and ruthless seduction, I was forced through embarrassment to row the river under whatever cover I could make for myself. I involved myself in voluntary overtime, I loitered by the playing fields until daylight sank into dusk. Finally the long evenings and British summertime defeated me. As I boldly launched myself one parched evening, she was sitting in the garden, drinking tea, stroking the cat in her lap, and catching the last heat from the sun. She had been playing tennis and was dressed for the part, good presentation being the essence of amateur participation in all sports. Her tennis racket was resting beside her chair. From the river I could see her marvellously tanned legs from knees to ankles and the peak of her white cap. I thought she would not see me. As my distracted oars clapped the water she stood alarmed and enraged by my chauvinistic discourtesy, dropping the cat, which growled at me and scampered to the shelter of the privet hedge, where better to ambush me. I smiled nervously and in return she turned in her baggy white shorts and walked to the house. With unusual zeal, I forced myself to tie up the boat. I could feel my heart as I climbed the low bank into her garden. The cat was spitting and I kicked a small stone hard into its midriff. In the corner of this painted lawn I was totally vulnerable. I knew from that moment she had won something from me, but as yet I was unaware of its value. The cat followed me warily, howling from the pit of its stomach.

The black interior, broken into small rectangles by the white undercoated, half-glossed window frames of the french window, threatened ominously. I shaded my eyes, but there were no signs, nor sounds of life from within. The paint was dry. I turned the handle, pulled the door and slipped inside as stealthily as, and with, a cat. The immediate smell was furniture polish, chilled wax rather than aerosol. Every item of furniture had a mahogany veneer and was highly polished. The application of chilled wax is more erotic than the labour of spraying. I stepped lightly across the floor, small influential landscape paintings littering the corners of my eyes. Three doors off this prominent room were all ajar, and, cautiously, I leant my ear against each in turn. The lack of noise echoed throughout the downstairs quarters. Narrow, open-sided stairs climbed out of this reception room into dark recesses aloft; miniature portraits ascended as dark brown rectangles. I stepped onto the lower staircase.

Tonight will be a long night. No company, the colour television in my wife's bedroom unwatchable through a tendency to red. The library book is outside in the rain. I make a sandwich from sanction-breaking tinned meat and spend an hour trying to percolate a decent cup of coffee, free from Kenyan grit.

As I turned half way up the stairs to mount the second half of the staircase, a small wedge of daylight from the room at the far end of the hall was the entire upstairs illumination. Never had I seen such a sun-neglected and dark interior. The bedroom doors were stained wood and the walls unornamented as a stark contrast to the downstairs decoration. A handle turned and her white silk figure leapt across the landing and disappeared into the steaming bathroom. She had not seen me in the shadows, but I almost turned on my heels out of alarm. Dampened music and whispered lyrics crept from the room she had quit, her bedroom so suddenly bathed in a white veil of natural light opened its door to me. My palms were sticky with sweat and a day's work. I was not sure why I was here or how I would explain my presence if discovered, or even how I could control my reactions on being uncovered by a hysterical female. Her vanity case was scattered across her bed, nearby her handbag and a glimpse of her red leather wallet. The relief of finding money to satisfy my corrupt desires was immense. I picked the purse, unloaded a tight fold of papermoney and left more swiftly than I had entered. Those few pounds financed the extravagances in the early days of our courtship.

★

From my bedroom next to hers at the back of the house, I hear a car pull to a halt at the bottom of the drive and see the main beam slowly fade. Another midnight has passed. I wait for the doors to slam. Several minutes elapse in departing conversations before I allow their lack of consideration to concern me. I can see nothing incriminating from the window, but a masochistic urge to be convinced of her infidelity and a reluctance to get wet in the rain were battling it out within me. I hear a car door closed with deliberate stealth and the car rolls away down the drive to the gate before engaging the engine. Obviously a deceit is being practised.

I lie on my single bed in the darkness fully clothed as security from the storm, which has bristled in the background all night. The area is susceptible to these lingering storms. Amateur meteorologists in the Cricketers blamed the local geography, a vast basin with tight valley exits. The whole concept, true or false, animated this meteorological phenomenon, now a cornered wild beast. I keep my clothes on, especially my shoes. When I was a child, I remember crying at the outset of a particularly severe storm. My mother took my hand and we stood in the bay window. She drew back the curtains and we shared a broad view of another valley. She pointed to the sky and told me to watch as the fearsome sulphurous balls of cloud moved away, how too the resonance of the thunderclap became less amplified. She held my hand and forced me to face up to my fears. I was terrified. I have always hated thunderstorms and self-analysis.

I must have fallen asleep quite soon, for I did not hear my wife come upstairs and she would certainly have looked into my room and disturbed me by switching on the light. She knew my abhorrence of electric storms. I awake at three a.m., according to the illuminated dial of my alarm clock, and conclude that she has paid her respects in silence and pressed gin-loaded lips to my cheek in pity. The storm has subsided, but though the night is still black it smells refreshed and green. Waking from sleep is a peculiar moment. Immediate problems are drowned in a sea of drowsiness, the lazy river of reality flowing outside this safe room, outside this house. The house is still dark and silent, 'merrily, merrily, merrily, merrily, life is just a dream.'

The strong morning sunlight lights my small bedroom. The plain white walls and thin curtains lend violent assistance to my awakening. I dress, wash, brush my teeth and go downstairs to make my breakfast. The air is clear and I feel lighthearted and happy until my nostrils are assailed by the smell of dead cats and cooked liver and I become incapable of ruining another day with bacon, eggs and indigestion. I make a jug of strong instant coffee and a pyrex pudding basin full of cornflakes. I intend eating in the open air to show my contempt for humdrum existence, but the garden chair is saturated and Hemingway uncommonly limp. I place the tray on the chair and squat before breakfast, adaptability being the keynote of happiness. I see a careless field-mouse and am reminded of the cat's demise. Behind me morning hopefuls are to-ing and fro-ing across the watermeadows. I am able to sneer at their aspirations and jealousies, with a clear conscience, only showing a broad back as a stream of milk dribbles from the upturned corner of my mouth into the slop of soggy cereal. After breakfast, I carry the tray into the kitchen and leave the dirty crockery on the draining board for my wife. A penance, if you like, for her night of pleasure; she has not yet stirred to her guilt. It is eleven o'clock, three by my alarm clock, and I decide cutting the lawn might effectively disturb her. I want to see regret in her alcohol-poisoned, hungover eyes. Half an hour later and the lawn is shaved into neat lines. I imagine her in her white nightdress looking down from somewhere up there, drinking alka-seltzer and squinting through the effervescence, pledging 'never again'. I notice that the helicopter patrols have stopped, but am not sure of the exact moment of their cessation. After cutting the grass, the absence of activity is intense. I put my ear to her door at 11.45 but no sound of regret comes to calm my neurosis.

Today is Thursday, not a special day, no anniversaries forgotten or to remember, but a day on which I have arranged to meet a distraction from my marital problems. She called herself Georgina now, or Geraldine to protect her reputation, as I walk her through the talkative watermeadows, beneath the scrutiny of the aerial patrols. I prefer home to consummate our affair, so as not to risk damp, grass-stained knees and rheumatism. To her credit, she has resisted my advances through six, evermore frustrating Thursday afternoons and a couple of spontaneous weekend encounters. I could only flatter myself by my persistence. Her defences had caved too late last week, too near my evening meal, too close to my return home to incite any response beyond a promise and a tick on the kitchen calendar.

Thus I take my life and my sports jacket in my hands and go out to meet her beneath a significant tree. Should her passion have cooled I can take her for a drink. My wallet is tidily concealed and I will waste an hour or so until our adrenalin has taken us back emotionally to the point of last week's parting. In these desperate early days of courtship, progression to the ultimate act must be steady, not of necessity hasty.

Georgina is waiting for me in a most unattractive tweed suit, with a large matching cap pulled down over one eye. She is circling the tree stealthily, carrying a tan shoulder bag, kicking leaves, pursing her lips, but not whistling. I am obviously late. I wait for her to see me, which gives me a chance to watch and be aware of changes in her mood. Visual contact established with a smile, I step forward, take her hand and kiss her on the cheek as the twisted brim of her cap obstructs a full-frontal attack. She is nervously excited, keen to tell me the news of the week in notation and I am equally keen to silence her. A patronizing laugh is noticed, but unheeded. The minutiae of her life is unendurable. I endure. She tells me there was a hive of activity below the waterworks. A gathering of gawping onlookers had emptied the footpaths of the watermeadows. An ambulance waited, rear doors wide and a panda car parked head on, blue lights barring the route of its exit. An obscure malady has stricken the typewriters in her office, she is the typist with a broken typewriter. However, her vocal chords clatter on with murderous mechanical efficiency. The typewriter mechanic mistyped 'the quick brown fox jumps over the lazy hen', distracted by the gossip and Geraldine's long, twisting legs.

We cross the bridge with tremendous courage and noticeable modesty; if Georgina is not shivering it is me. As we walk I persuade myself my marriage is over. I have not the slightest inclination to fight to prolong our relationship. Nevertheless I leave Georgina by the back gate, until I have reconnoitred the house in particular and the garden and distant horizon in general.

The downstairs has not been disturbed since my departure. My wife's room is forlorn rather than empty, although her clothes still force open the wardrobe doors and dressing-table drawers. I go into my room and look down on Georgina circling out of habit, head bowed unproudly. She carries her handbag in front of her knees like an impassable hurdle. I see no future out of this window.

I lead Geraldine by the hand through the dining room and upstairs to my bedroom, where to perform our ritual. I work against her ice-cold afternoon legs without music, although the helicopters are circling once again. Reaching and drained by a runaway ecstasy, I feel an ominous shadow, greater and more sinister than my wife's, urging me forward.

The helicopter is hovering in such close proximity that I barely hear the door chime. I depress my partner's shoulders, leaving her between death and indecision, and leap to my feet.

A heavyweight, round-shouldered, plainclothes policewoman and her spindly assistant obstruct the daylight when I open the door. The former tips her hat, while the latter opens a small pocket notebook and fumbles for a miniature pencil hidden in his breast pocket. The latter addresses me formally. I invite them into the kitchen and boil a kettle. He notes the state of the kitchen, dishes from a single breakfast unwashed, the feline corpse and the helicopter humming over our conversation. I had forgotten to put the cat out. They are asking about my wife's whereabouts in a roundabout manner. They have found a woman's body in the water about a mile downstream, with no marks on its person to suggest a struggle, but a damp red wallet and several items in the pockets. I offer them a gingernut with their coffee. Geraldine comes into the kitchen in one of my shirts and a tweed cap.

The helicopter crew had discovered the body earlier this morning and their immediate identification was greatly helpful to the police.

Georgina makes another coffee, cuts a Mr Kipling cake into four and scrapes a piece of half-eaten pig's liver into the flip-top kitchen bin.

Later in the day I hear that the police have arrested Martin. By evening rodents are seen crossing into the watermeadows from the sewage farm; in the morning they will be in my garden. In their eyes I will appear as a participant in a tableau representing paradise. By mid-morning in a particularly hot summer I, crosslegged in a canvas chair and unthreatening to their presence, sip chilled martini and lemon in the shade of an apple tree, a library book in my lap. That the garden seat is not specifically designed for their comfort and that the book, with its British Safety Standard seal of approval is by Hemingway, are facts not distantly apparent, nor of the remotest interest to a rat.

Hide and Seek

Graham Swift

There were always games. In the big, austere house on the outskirts of Inverness (built on the profits of a distillery in which Uncle Alex had owned a third share – though Uncle Alex was reputed never in his life to have drunk a drop of whisky) there was much, not least Uncle Alex himself, to forbid games. But in the circumstances – the special circumstances – he had allowed himself to soften. He had taken them into his home, two children who were not his own. And – no matter what a grave eye he cast upon the events that had brought them to him (it must have been a blow, a bitter blow for him too) – he had applied shrewd instinct and gentle tact. Let the children play, was his new-found, tacit motto. He opened his house suddenly to his neighbours' children too, so that, counting his own son and two daughters, there were sometimes nine or ten of them invited to amuse themselves under his roof. Let the children play, Uncle Alex enjoined. What these children most need now is to play. So that, yes, even then perhaps they had seen it: this formidable man, with his granite principles and his fixing gaze, he had been shaken, knocked just a little out of his mould, though he wouldn't admit it; he too (though it wasn't in him) would have liked to melt.

Only on Sundays when, with Uncle Alex and his wife and their three children, he and his sister would be taken to church, and then, after dinner, packed off to Sunday school, was the injunction to play suspended. Though then it would seem to him – had it also to Jean? – that what was involved was just another kind of game. Little rewards for remembering your Bible passage off by heart, little reminders that if you did

such-and-such you would be worthy of Jesus, but if you did
. . . And as for the Sunday morning services, what seemed to
matter was not the meaning, or efficacy, of minister McPhee's
sermons, which formed their centre-piece, but the ritual of
being there, to sing hymns and mouth prayers and go through
customary motions, the indescribably safe and forgetful feeling of being inside that cavernous, dim-lit building with its
arching membranes of stone, its brass-eagle lectern, its smell
of must and polish, with, outside, the exposed churchyard and
the open hills.

And hide-and-seek had been their favourite game. Was it
that Uncle Alex – this man who was not their father but who
stepped into the place of their father – had seemed at first, with
his bushy, steel-grey eyebrows and looming stature, someone
eminently to hide from? Just as it seemed that when they
assembled at church on Sundays it was in reality to hide from,
not to meet with, God. For whatever was said about the
church being God's house, it was surely a place of human
refuge, human closeness. God, if he was anywhere, was really
outside, a cold and scrutinizing presence, not unlike Uncle
Alex, waiting to break open this nest of holiness his worship-
pers had constructed.

Was it simply that the rambling house, with its attics and
cellars, its outhouses and grounds, was ideally suited to the
game? Or was it that hide-and-seek is one of those games
which plunges its participants inescapably into the realms of
primitive, desperate adventure?

He had always preferred hiding to seeking. Against the
shallow thrills of the hunt, there was no comparing that deep,
silent excitement of huddling in your place, of being suddenly
extinct, of listening to the sounds of the house, the scrambles
of other hiders, the footsteps on hallway or stair of whoever
was 'It', drawing close, retreating, approaching again. And
that other excitement – was it a kind of terror or ecstasy? – of
being discovered, the cupboard door flung open, the bed-
spread lifted, of being jerked back into bright daylight; as if it
were possible, just possible that in that incubatory period, that

spell of breathless detachment, the world might have changed and not be any more the one it was; or that you yourself might not be, might just not be, the person you had been; and hauled out, struggling in the triumphant grasp of 'It', might somehow be reborn.

An essay he had written as a student of psychology on the significance of children's games: hide-and-seek as a being and not-being game; a game in which we act out the notion of a world in which we do not exist, and likewise acknowledge a world which can exist without us; a game in which we observe the effect upon others of our own decease and, conversely, imitate, in the process of being 'found', the experience of 'being about to be'. . .

Hack stuff. Obvious, facile, quasi-Freudian stuff. Now, a practising psychoanalyst, though he wouldn't dispute the excitement – yes, the deep excitement – of those hide-and-seek games, he wouldn't ascribe to such bunk. So much of psychology seemed to him now hack, obvious stuff. Clever-talk. Making games out of games. Explanations that explained nothing. Like saying that the reason why, at forty-five, he still did not know whether he preferred men or women and was in other ways – to speak like a layman – a mess, was because when he was small his father had left his mother and then (he was eleven and Jean was twelve) his mother had committed suicide.

They had finished now. He had placed his wreath (how like a game this was too). There only remained the shovelling of earth onto the coffin. There would be no further formalities of gatherings. That was up to him, after all, as next of kin. He had paid for the funeral, so he called the tune. Besides, what kind of gathering could there be? He no longer belonged here. He had travelled overnight on the sleeper from London to attend this half-hour ceremony. Uncle Alex's house was now a hotel. He did not know the whereabouts of Uncle Alex's daughters; he had written to the son – in Canada. Uncle Alex and Auntie Ruth were under marble slabs in another part of the churchyard (only a two year interval between them he'd noticed) and perhaps by some means available to the dead they were now installing in their ghostly household the woman they had sheltered as a child.

He knew none of the handful of mourners who had turned up at the graveside. If one or other of Uncle Alex's daughters were among them, he did not recognize them – and they preferred to conceal their identities. Perhaps Jean had had friends he'd known nothing of. Or perhaps they were just local people who took a prying interest in this spinster who, though she had moved long ago to another part of Inverness, wished to be buried in their church. Perhaps they vaguely remembered the two orphan children – orphans in effect, at least – who had moved in with Alex McDonnell (an ugly sort of business – an unfaithful husband, a wife who'd taken an overdose). How the sister had stayed, at least in Inverness, but the brother had left. What did they know about him? That he was a psychiatrist in London. Nothing more? Enough. And perhaps their motives, after all, were kind; fond memory of his sister, sympathy for the bereaved brother. And perhaps at this moment they might be about to introduce themselves, convey condolences, say 'I knew Jean –', offer a little hospitality before his long journey back. Save that numerous, tentative glances, between him and them, them and him, glances which brought down unexpected shutters and caused uneasy fidgetings, had made it clear that here was a man who didn't want company right now, who didn't want to be approached or to revive old connections.

Perhaps, he suddenly thought with a chill sensation, these were the grown-up versions of those neighbourhood children with whom he, Jean and the McDonnells had played their therapeutic games. All the more reason. . .

So, no, there would be no post-funereal pleasantries. Except for the minister. The minister, who was very plainly turning towards him now, proffering again the large, bony, slightly hesitant hand he had already shaken once. The minister was bound to engage him in talk and press upon him some token courtesy. A glass of sherry or dram of whisky at the manse (but no, despite Uncle Alex's house being a hotel with a licensed bar, this was still a district where they mixed abstinence with affluence). Tea and sympathy then, with the minister's wife?

He could hardly escape the minister. And the minister knew he was a psychiatrist. And he could see that as he stepped towards him now he did so with that slight rigidity with which someone, no matter under what duty of compassion, steps towards a potential antagonist.

An image of his father framed still – framed for ever – in the window of the Inverness train inside which he and Jean were seated. A blurred, imperfect image (he had not known it was the last time he would see him, so why should he have made a point of remembering?) But he recalled a man trying desperately hard to be kind, to be clearly, manifestly their father, effusive in his concern at seeing them off on this journey – Edinburgh to Inverness – which was still a long journey for two small children to make for themselves. So fussy and solicitous that he'd embarrassed them before the other passengers. Must he make it all so obvious? Must he spoil the fact that they were about to depart on a long journey by themselves and were perfectly grown-up enough to accomplish it? For that was what that journey had meant to him; evidence that he was grown-up, when you did things for yourself. And he was going to manage it, and make chivalrously sure that Jean was all right.

Their father mouthed things that were blotted out by the station sounds and the noise of escaping steam. He had bought them sandwiches, lemonade, sweets, comics. He had bought him a brand new book; an illustrated child's version of the legends of King Arthur – knights, damsels, enchanted forests. He'd said, 'Mummy will be there when it gets in,' and, 'I'll be with you on Saturday.' He eyed his watch. And then when the train pulled out he began to wave furiously and grotesquely; his last words were all but lost.

Was it mere fancy to see, now, in that image through the train window a vision of a man floundering, drowning? Or to imagine that he was trying – at the very last moment – to explain? But before the train outpaced him, his shouted words reached them. They were directed at Jean; and they stung the pride of her chivalrous companion.

'Look after him, Jean!'

And so, on the sleeper from London; dreams – such dreams! Dreams of trains and knights in armour. But forget the hack interpretation of dreams.

'Doctor Grant, at least allow my wife and I to offer you a little hospitality.'

He explained that he must leave at once. If he was to get the train from Inverness in time for the southbound sleeper. His work in London. He had to be there in the morning.

The minister paused. He must know it was possible to get a later train to Edinburgh and still make the overnight to London.

'Well let me ring for a taxi for you – and while you wait – '

'That's all right, thank you. I'll walk to the hotel and ring for one there.'

'The hotel?'

'Yes.'

'Oh, I see, you want . . . of course.'

Yes, he might take a look. But there was a bar there too, which was more to the point, and it would be open in half an hour.

'Would you mind then – if I walked with you?'

He was pressing the point. There was something in it for him. Some sort of challenge. He couldn't refuse.

'No.'

'If we slip through the church first. I must – ' (he hesitated, indicating the large Bible he was carrying, no doubt to a psychiatrist it was all fairy tales) ' – put this back where it belongs.'

He hesitated again, more solemnly. They were still near the grave. Wouldn't he want a last look? A last moment of silent, meditative respect? And then he saw clearly the keen-faced minister's view of him; the cold man of science, the soul dissector, with no time for the ceremonials of death, or even good, plain, honest emotion.

And if he'd scarcely paid her a visit while she was alive . . ?

'Or I could meet you here again?'

'No, that's all right. I'll come through the church.'

They walked towards the side entrance. He didn't turn his head – as if deliberately to fail the minister's test.

And then, inside, while the minister left him for a while, it was suddenly, even without the hymn singing and the McDonnells sitting in a row in the pew, just as it used to be: the enclosure, the feeling of removal. He wanted to cry out. And when the minister rejoined him and they walked out, there was the same feeling he'd had on those Sundays long ago – that the bright, insistent morning might no longer be there.

It took nearly half an hour, or so he remembered, from the church back to Uncle Alex's. For a minute or so they walked in difficult silence. Then the minister began, 'Your sister – you understand, I never knew her, but when I was informed of her death, some of the older residents told me about – the connection. Your sister, she never married?'

No, she never did. More hack explanations for that too. Because when she was a girl her father left her mother, so she had a reason to hate husbands. Moreover, as a result her mother took her life, and there, all ready and neat, was the subconscious formulation: my father killed my mother.

Did the minister know the facts? He must do – wasn't it the

cheap intrigue of it all that was prompting these questions? That, and the notion that people turn to ministers – or psychiatrists.

The find-out-why game, the you-can-tell-me game.

You can accept that stock shrink's explanation, if you like. Her father killed her mother. Ergo, men were her enemy. Ergo, she had to avoid them.

Or you can go a bit deeper. She had to find a way of bearing it all. She had to find a way of, though she was in the world, getting away from it. Going inward, going into hiding. Being and not being.

A recluse in an Inverness mansion block, whom – even when she succumbed to a fatal disease – her cold-hearted little brother would scarcely visit.

But you see, minister, I don't care for all these theories. All this stuff from my student days I regurgitate when I can't think of anything else.

I hope when we get there the bar's open.

And there was more than one way. But the first way – it isn't done.

Suicide, too, isn't done, but is. That Saturday he never turned up. He'd got a train to London, or wherever, to join his other woman. There was a letter from him on the following Monday. And then, four weeks after that, Mother was dead – it was the same recourse her daughter adopted, only more extreme (people call it a Way Out) – and we were suddenly one hell of a problem for Uncle Alex.

'No, she never married. She had the example of her, that is, our mother's marriage. You know, I suppose – ?'

The minister gave a discreet glance.

'I buried the McDonnells, Doctor Grant. It was one of my first – sad – duties as new minister.'

And the glance took on, just for an instant, it seemed, a disapproving edge. A thrust? That he hadn't turned up to

Uncle Alex's funeral (had Jean then?) – had neglected the man who had been like a second father. It confirmed the rumours. London. Psychiatry (Alex McDonnell could never make out the lad). While here in good old sober Inverness . . .

'And you – ' the minister went on ' – you never married?'

So he did know. Rumours . . .

No, never. If you cannot decide whether you prefer men or women, it's a bit difficult to enter wedlock. If your life has been peppered with short-lived and furtive affairs with one sex or another, it's a bit difficult to think of permanent conjugality. He'd hoped once that one day he'd make up his mind (if his mind had anything to do with it), and that, to make things simpler, it would be women. Just as he'd hoped once, while the other hope faded, that psychiatry would provide him with that vital thing: an enlightened viewpoint. But he'd never made up his mind. And now it was too late. Because the fact was he'd become addicted to this process of continuous and disastrous experimentation, of grubbing about – privately and professionally – in other people's lives.

Though I don't believe any more, minister, in psychiatric enlightenment, in all the psychoanalytical answer books. If you want my professional opinion, they're all hogwash. God knows what makes people tick. I only believe – and it's what keeps me in my consulting room – that people want to *tell*. They want to confess. It's the hardest thing in the world to do, but they want to do it. They want to open their mouths and let something they could never calculate saying, they could never believe themselves saying, come out. And I'm afraid – since I'm with you, minister – they prefer not to do it, on the whole, with Bibles and sermons thrown in and the problem of their souls in the next world. But they want this thing so much that they'll pay large sums of money for it. Just for someone to listen . . .

★

'No, I never married either. Tell me, how long has my late uncle's house been a hotel?'

He wanted to change the subject. To get away from this minister's faintly condescending, faintly sympathetic, faintly prurient line of inquiry.

'When Mr and Mrs McDonnell died,' (the minister concealed annoyance at being diverted) 'the son – '

'James – '

' – the one who went to Canada – sold it to a developer who wanted to make it into a hotel.' He paused, a little uneasily. 'I don't know, of course, if he knew that was the intention when he sold it.'

'But none the less a hotel it became.' (And there it was before them now, emerging round the bend in the road, the 'Glenavon', lounge bar and all, where once Uncle Alex, with his whisky shares, had drunk nothing stronger than tea or coffee.) 'My uncle Alex,' he wanted to say, 'would have turned in his grave', but saw that that would scarcely have been appropriate.

But the minister caught his meaning.

'Mr McDonnell was a sad loss – a fine, strong man, a respected man.'

Yes – and a man who knew a cure: Let the children play.

Though when is a game no longer a game? It became clear, by their second year in the house, that 'play' was not all it was. Clear, not so much to Uncle Alex, who had become so seduced by his own system of therapy (a houseful of childish frolicking, no time for them to sit and brood) that he had forgotten that a cure is not an end but a means; but clear to Jean, who could not help noticing his sharpening interest in the McDonnell daughters, just as he could not help noticing (there had been a painful period when he had no counter-interest to pull her back) her interest in James McDonnell and in Peter Stevens and Tom Balfour.

But 'interest' wasn't the word. It wasn't attraction. It was fear. Or (but no hack explanations) guilt at a frowned-upon attraction (steely-browed Uncle Alex watching, like God, even if he did not see). He was suddenly afraid of those two sisters and of the other girls who before had been his unexceptionable playmates. When he hid and they found him or when they hid and he was obliged to find them, the moments of discovery seemed to demand an extra heed, as if another game, a game within a game (he preferred to find or be found by James McDonnell or Tom Balfour), were being set in motion.

It was hurting them, him and Jean, it was making them desperate, this sense of enticement which wasn't, for some reason, simple for them. It reminded them that they were still a separate, alien community of two in this land of adoption. They would never learn its customs. And perhaps it was this desperation that made it happen, paradoxically, so much quicker, go so much further with them.

A way of going inward . . .

It was January. Snow was falling in thick flakes outside. In one of the attic rooms was an old stout deal table, shrouded with a large, moth-eaten, red-plush Edwardian table-cover. They never intended to hide together. But they'd both headed for the upper rooms – they had this way of shadowing each other, as if to save the other from harm – and when he'd made for the draped table and lifted up the cover (it was an obvious hiding place but for that reason often overlooked) he'd turned to Jean in the doorway and said, 'Jean?'

The attic was unheated. The snowy light invaded the room through a dormer window and penetrated in flushed patches the threadbare portions of the table-cover. It was cold. He said to Jean, 'Jean, I'm cold. Are you cold?' And then because they'd huddled close, on the pretext of being cold, they'd discovered that, within this hiding place though they were, where no one could see them, there were layers on layers of other hidden and secret things to be uncovered. They could have stopped, either could have refused. But it was as though they were compelled to do this thing which in one sense they did not want to do, which they could never have imagined themselves doing, as some form of exquisite, punitive humiliation. In the middle of it they had both begun to cry – the tears of guilty, childish wrong-doers. She brought him to a weeping, moaning climax. No sexual experience would ever compare with it. But it was she who stopped weeping first. She wiped away his sperm with her handkerchief, like a mother wiping the tears of a baby. As if she were already slipping back into the role of the knowing, the capable elder sister – removing traces, coping with aftermaths, looking after little brother. As if her grown-up answers were already forming: This has happened, but only once, and it won't, shan't ever happen again. I renounce it, disown it, pretend it isn't there, shut it up inside of me for ever.

Hiding, hiding – in another way.

And he never found out what she did with that handkerchief soaked in his puerile seed. Tom Balfour was coming up the stairs, starting his search. He ran to a hiding place of his own. And from that day on all he wanted was to do it with her in the proper way, like he'd heard about.

To tell, minister, they want to tell.

And I want to tell you my sister was a good woman, a fine, strong woman . . .

She sat opposite him, facing the engine, upright and alert, not looking at the comics and books and scarcely stirring in her seat, while he lost himself with knight errants in magic forests and almost forgot the gallantry he owed his sister – the responsibilities he owed himself – on this other journey by train. So that when he looked up, her eyes, watching him as if they had been watching him for a long time, suddenly checked and shamed him. 'Look after him, Jean.' He put down his book, tried to act like a practised citizen of the real world of railway travel. He opened the bag of sandwiches. 'Hungry?' But she didn't want to eat. Her eyes turned to the snow-clad hills of passing Perthshire.

And later, much later, she told him, 'I knew, I knew all the time.'

So all through that railway journey he was in fantasy land anyway. Wanting to rebut his father's words, to show that he needed no looking after, while she already guessed beyond them and taking it all upon herself, not flinching or shirking, but already learning to put her feelings where no one else could reach them, wanted to spare him the knowledge.

'I knew. I knew all the time.'

That had been years afterwards, when he was about to depart for London – shunning the good, solid medical schools of Edinburgh and the prospect of becoming a good, solid Highlands doctor (Uncle Alex, beneath the censorious frowns, indulging a sigh of relief; the lad was getting into strange ways. But psychiatry? So what did he want – to explain himself?).

'I knew he would never come back to Inverness.'

She'd left it all those years and until the station buffet at Edinburgh to say it.

A perfectly gauged body blow? Because it was right here that *he* – ? And now he was leaving her – and *he*'d deserted Mother. And – perhaps she guessed it too, a second time – he was never going to return either.

And just to let him know, on top of all that, that he'd never been more than a child. To show him that she'd been, all along – still was – his protectress, had always been sitting in that railway seat, facing the engine, stronger than him, knowing what he didn't know. So, he was setting off to see the world, to find his own path just as, then, she'd let him read his fairy tales. But where did he think the hard truth was? And where did he think the one who knew better was? And he couldn't ever leave her, really, could he? Do without her, really, could he?

So run along, Dougie. Run and play your games. But some day you'll come back to find me.

And the fact was that he preferred hiding to seeking. He always wanted to be a hider not a seeker . . .

★

The snow was even thicker, the cold even more bitter (a ten degree frost), and this time it was early evening and already dark, when he hid in Uncle Alex's woodshed. That was six weeks after – Since when, no word, no sign, no hint of consequences. The answer, the stupid, grown-up answer: don't speak of it, don't show it, cover it up. When your father leaves you, when your mother – Act as if it never really – Bury it.

But now he was hiding, with chattering teeth, in the woodshed, to make his sister relent, repent – admit . . .

On such dark, frozen evenings, of course, they never played outside the house. But that was the point. Now his sister was 'It' she would find him – but only slowly, and not before she became scared, terrified, panic-stricken that he was lost. Not before she discovered how much it meant to him that she didn't want . . . wouldn't let him . . . not before he'd hurt her.

But it wasn't easy. It took courage and strength. It took iron strength and resolution to endure the cold of the woodshed. You wouldn't believe a woodshed could be so cold. It took courage not to yield when the distant voices could be heard calling – Jean's amongst them – with the unmistakable tones of mounting alarm. 'Come out, Dougie! Come out! The game's finished.' He crawled between two piles of logs. He knew there were bits of sacking, bundles of newspapers in the woodshed with which he could have wrapped himself – but this was not the point. The point was that he should be seen to have spurned suffering for the sake of some motive greater than the desire to escape suffering. The point was that this was not a game.

But it took courage to spurn suffering. It took courage to persist, even beyond that pitch where, had he returned to the house of his own accord, his point would have been made – it would have been clear this was no game.

Voices from within the house. Perhaps it had not occurred to them that he could be outside. Yet he had to go through with this action which it was surely within his will to stop at any time. It was when he realized that a time must come when, if he did not return indoors, he might become incapable of doing so – but still his will made no response – that he knew there were things deeper than courage, strength and will-power. Doing what isn't done. He crouched between the log piles. More voices. Jean's voice. 'A game in which we act out the notion of a world in which we do not exist . . . a game in which we observe the effect . . .'

The cold seemed no longer outside him, but part of him, in him. He smiled. He might have been found with a frozen smile upon his face.

But he'd been discovered (a desperate late-night search of the outhouses, with torches and bicycle lamps), pulled back, not with smiles but with screams, into the world again. Oh, the agony of it, the agony of thawing, coming to life again; there is no agony like it.

But did he get what he wanted? Did Jean give in? To cease to be and be born again, for Jean? Uncle Alex intervened.

'There'll be no more games in this house – no more hide-and-seek, not after this.'

Behind his authoritarian bulk Jean took cover. Perhaps it was the wrong way round. Perhaps it was she who should have hidden in the woodshed and he who should have found her. Perhaps she was an infinitely more adept, infinitely more courageous hider than he. Yes, and perhaps, against his will, he was a seeker – the baffled, the excluded one. Did she relent? No, it made things final, unrepealable, like Uncle Alex's prohibition of games. He would feel guilty for ever now for her isolation, her withdrawal. To freeze yourself is no way of making another melt.

'I sometimes think she might have been a nun.'

'Your sister?' The minister's eyes alerted at this gesture to his sphere of interest.

'That hermit's life of hers, living alone.' (And unvisited.) 'But then – I only speak as a layman – one shouldn't take up holy orders, should you, merely to reinforce a disposition, a way of life? It seems to me that if my sister had become a nun, that would only have been another – a more extreme – form of hiding.'

'Hiding? I can't allow that, Doctor Grant. What you call "hiding" I would call a kind of facing up.'

Facing up? So that's what she'd been doing. And he – ?

They drew near the hotel. With its name in large white letters over the ground floor windows and its clutter of signs and stickers around the entrance, it looked as if it had always been a hotel, not a home where once . . .

Was it possible that it was all, still, somehow, *in* there?

'What the world tends to regard nowadays, Doctor Grant, as hiding – escaping, retreating – isn't that at all. It's a way of making contact with another world. It's a way of acknowledging we don't wholly belong to this world.'

He seemed flustered, awkward. It was what he would be expected to say. It was his stock-in-trade. And yet it was as if it had been elicited out of him, against his will, as if he didn't really believe it, by this man (trained in eliciting) walking at his side.

Theological hogwash.

They had reached the hotel forecourt and come to a halt. A prickly silence.

'Minister – I've a little time. Can I buy you a drink?'

A test? Like the minister's in the churchyard? A provocation? For his uneasy piety, his own uneasy profanity?

'Thank you – no.'

Because he didn't drink? Because he drank, but not at lunchtime in the Glenavon Hotel? Because he drank, but not with a psychiatrist from London (bereaved though he was) of whom there were rumours and whom he must regard as a Spiritual Enemy?

The large, bony hand was suddenly thrust out again. A switch to his graveside, church-porch manner.

'I'll leave you then, Doctor Grant. Once more, my sympathies. I am glad to have met you – sorry, that the circumstances – I wish you a good journey.'

He turned and walked back the way they'd come with a distinct air of regained composure.

He entered the hotel. He found the bar and ordered a large whisky. Then another. . . . He resisted reconnoitring the hotel passageway and lobbies. Was it possible he might be recognized? That one of the staff? Or the very walls might cry out? He engaged the barman in talk. Talk, listen, draw them out. The barman had a certain expression . . . a flicker?

He did not ring for a taxi. There was ample time for the later train. He knew there had been another route to the church – seldom used by them when they strode out in their Sunday best – along a lower road, then by a path up the hill, to the edge of the churchyard. He was drunk enough now, stepping out of the hotel, not to mind. And if they saw him, he didn't care either. He didn't care if the minister saw him, eyes trained on him from some spyhole in the church. Let them all see him. Let them have this last morsel of a story. So he came back, to look again at her grave. The prodigal's remorse.

He found the lower road, found the path, asphalted and with a signpost, freshly painted, to the church. He climbed up it, panting through the patches of bracken and gorse, watching the church tower jut above the brow. Where the path stopped, at a gateway in the lower wall of the churchyard, he stopped too. From here the ground sloped up towards the church on the ridge, and you could see all the graves without stepping further. Jean's was now completely filled – the gravediggers had gone – and a mound of earth, the headstone and his wreath marked the spot. Now nothing else could happen. First there had been Jean, then there was a coffin, then a stone which would weather and a heap of soil which would grass over. Traces removed.

It was too plain, too obvious not to be deliberate. He stood at the gateway while the tears flowed (ah, the agony) down his face.

Jean, stop playing. Jean come out now. Come out.

Late Flowering

Peter Parker

She had said it at the school play.

'You're going to be a very beautiful old man,' she had said, rubbing in a white smear of grease-paint down the side of his nose. Catterick had looked forward to this production with a keen anxiety he could no longer sense, it seemed so much a part of youth. Other boys scanned the notice boards every Friday after lunch to see whether they had been chosen to play in a school team on the following day. They would crowd around the wooden-framed boards in the cloisters, where stray notices were pinned to the green baize like litter on a lawn. The captain of games would stride along, an adult amongst children, and pin up the pieces of paper in an orderly row. After he had left, the crowd would surge back again, jostling, ducking, standing on tiptoe. Those omitted from the teams would stroll away with forced nonchalance, attempting to hide their disappointment. Those chosen would whoop for joy and noisily congratulate each other. But Catterick would not be amongst the crowd, showing a lack of interest in games which his housemaster found disturbing. Catterick waited for one notice each term; the cast list of the forthcoming school play.

And there was no doubt about it, the boy could act. In the classroom and around the house he was quiet, serious and intelligent, not especially popular. As the preparations for the dress rehearsal of *The Tempest* – a most unsuitable choice – were underway, the housemaster was trying to put into words his opinion of Catterick for the end-of-term report.

'A sensible boy,' he wrote, 'and a useful member of the house. His health, once more, has let him down, and he has not been seen much on the games fields.' Then, as a balance to this lukewarm account, he added, 'I enjoyed his performance in the school play immensely.' The housemaster hoped that he would.

She had been an under-matron at the sanitorium, an old, red-bricked building which stood at the end of the long school drive. Mr Catterick could not remember her name, although he could clearly recall the tone of her voice, with its soft Scots accent. She had offered to help with the make-up because she disliked sewing. Other matrons and masters' wives wielded scissors and needles, ingeniously transforming old dresses, blankets and curtains to provide costumes. It had been rumoured that she had her eye on the producer, a young bachelor who taught history, and hoped that her efforts would bring forth praise and admiration, something her needlework would not do. However, when she was applying the broad, garish strokes of age to Catterick, her attention was concentrated upon him alone. Catterick was embarrassed by her proximity and tried to avoid her gaze, casting his eyes up towards the ceiling or down towards the floor. When she told him that he was going to be a very beautiful old man, he blushed beneath the pancake and muttered a grateful acknowledgement. At the same time he had thought: why can't I be a beautiful young boy? This would have been much more useful to him than such vague prophecies, and given him the confidence he so painfully lacked. Only on stage, camouflaged by make-up and costume, assuming the guise of somebody else, could he become extrovert and attractive. He was more relaxed and graceful when performing than ever he could be in normal life. He forgot that his hands were large, that one ear stuck out rather, that his eyes were too small. He simply acted, the gestures natural and expansive, the words pouring from him without hesitation.

'E. C. M. Catterick as Prospero,' ran the review in the school magazine above the signature 'Thespis', 'evidently had a clear understanding of his part, and communicated this to the audience with noteworthy maturity. The Epilogue was spoken beautifully, and no-one could refuse so eloquent and deserved an appeal for applause. J. R. Smethwick made a pert Miranda. . .'

Mr Catterick wondered whether he might have made a career in the theatre. It would have been insecure, no doubt, but it would not have been stultifying. His father would have disapproved, but at such a distance this obstacle seemed very small indeed. His father had died during the war, his mother during the early fifties. He had pleased them both by entering his uncle's firm of solicitors, working hard, and marrying at the sensible age of twenty-six.

'Don't rush into things,' his father had said on that embarrassing evening shortly after Catterick had left school. 'You're a level-headed lad; try to stay that way. Your mother and I have been very happy together, very happy. There *are* women who . . . well, I'm sure you know what I mean.' Catterick did not. 'You've all your life ahead of you, Edgar,' his father had continued, pouring another glass of whisky and handing it to his son, 'so don't go spoiling it by being impulsive. There's someone out there, you know, and one day you'll meet, and you'll *know*. Because she's been waiting for you just as you've been waiting for her. Now, when do you start at Uncle Roger's?'

When Catterick met Emily Stourton he did not get the impression that she had been waiting for him. He did not *know*. But he was attracted by her softness, by her abundant hair and by her reserve. He did not rush into marriage. Indeed, his courtship was so dilatory that Emily Stourton was taken completely by surprise when he announced his intentions. Whilst not exactly casual, his proposal lacked the sort of ardour usually associated with such requests. Emily Stourton, although disappointed by the manner, was pleasantly surprised by the matter, and accepted. While Catterick proposed he was thinking how eminently sensible he was being, asking so suitable a woman to marry him, but also how clumsy he was being in making his intentions known.

The wedding was quiet, everyone agreeing that the bride

and groom made a very nice couple. The honeymoon was also quiet. On the first night they lay side by side in the large bed in a Cornish hotel, both very tired. However, custom overcame fatigue, and they moved hesitantly together towards the middle of the bed and consummation. He was gentle and she was grateful, their lovemaking considerate, almost polite. Afterwards, she rested her head upon his chest, weeping quietly, relieved at casting off the burden of her virginity, and thankful that it had not been painful. He had one arm about her shoulder and lay back gazing up into the darkness towards the ceiling, aware of the dampness of her tears on his skin. He understood her weeping and did not interfere, for he too felt the melancholia which hung around the room. He knew then the inadequacy of language which left them both tearful and silent until they slept.

They spent their days walking along the beach, he in grey flannel trousers and a Fairisle pullover, she in a neat, slim frock, just like any other couple of the period. Catterick's complexion coloured in the sun and wind, and his stride lost its gangling hesitancy. Emily clung to him, unsteady on the shingle, screwing up her face against the breeze. They sat under the cliffs on a plaid travelling rug, given to them by one of Emily's sisters, eating packed lunches provided by the hotel. Emily read whilst Catterick watched seabirds through an old pair of binoculars which he carried on a brown leather strap around his neck. Occasionally Emily would read out a sentence which amused her, and Catterick would point to a group of gulls pattering along the foreshore. They took tea at the various tearooms in the town, always choosing plain scones with jam and cream. They dined out once or twice, but decided that their hotel provided the best dinner. Every other night they had a bottle of wine with their meal.

They undressed in the dark, not talking, hearing only the soothing, regular rush of the sea outside and the rustle of falling clothes within. Once in bed they were nervously garrulous, recalling details of the previous day as they lay apart. Then they fell silent, shifting positions, limbs brushing each other almost by accident; but instead of recoiling, they remained touching. Tentatively he would reach out a hand to touch her shoulder as if guiding her towards him, and she would respond, slowly, until they met, silent beneath the sheets.

After his marriage Catterick seemed to forget about the smallness of his eyes and that one ear stuck out more than the other. His hands were in proportion now that he was mature. He was happy at work and at home, and simply forgot his adolescent worries. No-one would have said that he and Emily were *radiantly* happy, for their contentment was placid and turned inwards. They did not talk about their marriage when in company, or walk around showing off their status as if trying to sell it to others. They had not been extrovert before their partnership, and were not so after it. There had been no chemical reaction, no fireworks. Two inert substances had come together to form an involatile compound. Outsiders might have seen them together and imagined them bored with each other's company, but Catterick's parents looked on and nodded wisely. Catterick's housemaster, now retired to a small cottage in Shepton Mallet, would have reflected with satisfaction that the child is father to the man.

Several years of passive contentment passed, during which only relatives were concerned that Emily showed no signs of pregnancy. Catterick's father said to his wife that young people wanted to establish themselves before starting a family, and that she wasn't to fret. Catterick's work in the solicitors' office pleased his uncle.

'You ought to be proud of your son,' he said to his brother, a remark he repeated often because his own son was a disappointment and had run away to Canada with an older woman. 'Good job, good marriage, good prospects.'

By the time war broke out, Emily was still without children, and thirty-three years old. People began saying that it was very sad, and would make for a lonely old age. Catterick's father remarked that it would be hardly right to bring children into the world at the present moment, the international situation being what it was. Catterick, at thirty-four, was neither old nor beautiful but, as far as he could tell, he was functioning perfectly well. Neither he nor Emily talked about their lack of progeny, or thought to do anything about it. Both imagined that it was a matter of continuing as they were, patient and affectionate.

Catterick took a desk-job for the duration of the war, handling confidential documents with thoroughness but without curiosity. The Ministry was sorry to see him go when peace was restored, but Catterick felt a duty towards his uncle, especially after his own father died. The feeling that in some arcane way he had been doing something positive towards an Allied victory during the war made Catterick's work back at the solicitors' office seem trivial and routine. He was conscientious, efficient and bored.

It became clear that Emily was not going to bear any children, and there was no Catterick Senior to reassure people that all was well. Neither Catterick nor his wife would have considered apportioning blame, and they simply and tacitly resigned themselves to the fact that they would leave no heirs. It was probably time more than childlessness that deadened the marriage. They had come together to give each other confidence. Whilst it could not be said that either of them *blossomed* during the early years of their marriage, neither was the stiff, aloof personality of pre-wedding days. In the years before the war the marriage had spent itself, having given all it had to give. A child might have revitalized the union, but chiefly because it would have been a distraction. All that was left was companionship, and that proved not to be enough. By the time he was forty-five Emily no longer enhanced Catterick's life, and the benefits of the marriage had worn off. They slept apart and Catterick grew a beard.

Then Emily died of a heart complaint. Catterick buried his wife with dignity and regret. He had been surprised by the suddenness of her death, and was sorry that the relationship had foundered. It did not occur to him to remarry, for he was a person ideally suited to widowhood. He had come into his estate, almost as if he had married simply in order to become a widower. He was fifty-two. Lines marked his face, around the small eyes and across his forehead. He stared into the mirror each morning trying to determine which lines were permanent, and which were the result of tiredness, and would vanish. He checked his hairline, which was not receding, and wondered whether to shave off his beard. Not yet, he thought, not yet; for I am only in my fifties.

Whilst in the park, eating the sandwiches he made for his lunch each day, he studied old people, trying to guess their ages. He decided that one would have to be seventy before being classed as really old. Some people aged more quickly than others, but he never looked older than he was. Like fine whisky, he thought, I'm maturing slowly. The government classed one as old at sixty-five; or rather they classed one as 'senior', a supposedly comforting euphemism borrowed no doubt from America. Catterick had watched a television programme about plastic surgery in California, 'a land of desperate Dorian Grays', as the commentator put it. A seedy-looking Englishman had interviewed men and women who were relying upon doctors to erase the signs of age from their faces. These people were paying a great deal of money for operations which looked very uncomfortable. When the bandages had been removed and the bruises had gone, the faces looked as clean and blank as a wiped slate. The Californians seemed pleased with the results. And so now, thought Catterick, I will not become an old age pensioner, but will be given the spurious dignity of the term 'senior citizen'. Middle-aged women would start grabbing his arm to guide him across streets, people would offer him seats on public transport, distant relatives would start making discreet enquiries about the local meals-on-wheels service. People would not understand that Catterick's entire life had been one of anticipation, and that it was in old age that he would flourish, bloom and have his days of glory.

At sixty-five Mr Catterick retired from his job, without regrets. He had never become a senior partner, but had continued to work steadily and diligently, so that many of the firm's clients stipulated that they wished him to deal with their problems, and no-one else. Mr Catterick was gratified, but was relieved to be free of the office, his only worry being that he might have to wait up to ten years before attaining beauty. What if his mind gave out before the time was up? His health was good for he had never over-exerted himself in youth, had eaten sensibly, drunk moderately and smoked not at all. He had walked to work and back every day, and at weekends had travelled into the countryside to stride over the hills. He had every intention of being in a fit condition to enjoy his season. He had spent little money, partly because he had no dependants, but principally because he realized that money would be a bulwark against various parties who regarded lack of means as an excuse for interference. Mr Catterick greatly looked forward to the day when the social services came scrabbling and whining at his front door like terriers at a fox's earth. He planned to treat them with the disdain he usually reserved for doorstep evangelists. No, thank you, he did not require a local schoolchild to do his shopping for him. Whether or not his fuel bills were paid up to date was not a matter he wished to discuss with complete strangers. Not today, thank you. Good-day.

One day Mr Catterick shaved off his beard, and noted with satisfaction that the lines upon his face were becoming more numerous, and more deeply etched. His face was thinning, making his cheekbones more prominent, and his nose seemed sharper. He began taking off his clothes. He unbuttoned his shirt, then walked over to the window and drew the curtains. If anyone saw a man of sixty-eight removing his clothes in the middle of the day there would be vans at the door within the hour as the whole weight of the welfare state swung into action. Mr Catterick turned on the light in his bedroom, then carefully took off his trousers, which he folded neatly and hung over the back of a chair. He took off his shirt, his vest, his pants and his socks, and stood in front of the full-length mirror. He was content with what he saw. Never having bothered to build up his muscles in youth, he did not have the problem of their sagging from disuse in age. His belly was almost trim and he did not have drooping buttocks or breasts. His knees were not particularly knobbly and all seemed to be in proportion, although his calves were rather bulbous, no doubt the result of his long walks. His genitals hung neatly beneath a neat grey bush of pubic hair, which did not fan up unattractively all over the stomach. They did not look gnarled and gross or shrivelled and useless. He was not reminded of a poulterer's shop window. Some men had hair all over them, he reflected. One saw them on beaches, a thick, grey fluff on their shoulders. He was grateful that he was not the satyrlike type. As he pulled on his clothes once more, Mr Catterick remarked to himself that he was almost there.

Mr Catterick read a great deal, particularly enjoying anthropological volumes which he borrowed from the local library. He read of ancient civilizations, and of tribes which still existed, where the old were revered without qualification.

''E's always borrowing them books about darkies,' said one librarian as she watched Mr Catterick enter the building. 'Lives all by 'isself.'

'No family?' asked another librarian.

'No. Wife died ever so young. No kiddies. Sad, innit?'

Mr Catterick asked the librarians to recommend any books about old age. They directed him to a small section where he found two books about geriatric nursing, a volume entitled *Winter of Their Discontent*, several dealing with sexual offences and the rehabilitation of criminals, and, inexplicably, a collection of writings by lesbians. None of these appealed to Mr Catterick, so he borrowed a book called *Amongst the Ibo* instead. He also read the Bible; not for religious enlightenment, but because it contained so many salutary accounts of the extremely aged. Here were cricket scores indeed; Noah out for 950, Abraham reaching 175.

When not reading, he took the bus out of town into the open countryside. He remembered his honeymoon and the walks along the beach with Emily, when they had been young and tentative. As he walked, he planned. Soon he would be seventy and it would be time to emerge, for however brief a moment, from the chrysalis that had been his life. He would shed the unimaginative respectability he had gained, would stretch his wings, would challenge, would take risks. And yet, despite such aspirations, Mr Catterick was unsure about the exact form all this would take. But he was not impatient, he had time.

Mr Catterick took a large, striped towel from the airing cupboard, folded it and rolled it up. It was one of a pair that he and Emily had been given as a wedding present by a cousin, since deceased. Mr Catterick reflected that a great many of those wedding presents had outlived their donors, as indeed had he. He wondered what had happened to the under-matron who had so accurately predicted his late flowering. He supposed that she was dead as well. He put the rolled-up towel into a deep basket, then went downstairs to make sandwiches.

It was Mr Catterick's seventy-first birthday. To mark the fact, the postman had delivered a single card. It had a flower embossed upon it, perhaps a rose, with *Happy Birthday* picked out in gold lettering. Inside there was a verse:

> Although the years may vanish
> Just like the Morning's dew,
> Passing Time won't banish
> My kindly thoughts of You.

Underneath was written in an unsteady hand: 'Hope you are keeping well? With best wishes from Sybil Bailey.' Mr Catterick had not the faintest idea who Sybil Bailey might be, but he received a card from her every year. He wondered whether she was a relative of Emily. There was never any address, so he could not reply even if he had wanted to. He did not like the idea of a total stranger being in possession of his address, and occasionally he would worry that Sybil Bailey would arrive on his doorstep one afternoon with a suitcase and good intentions. No-one else ever sent him a card. He wondered whether the people who used to remember his birthday had decided one year not to bother, or whether they had simply died.

Mr Catterick cut a pile of sandwiches in half with a large, sharp breadknife, then wrapped them in greaseproof paper. He poured some strong tea into a thermos flask and screwed on the lid firmly. From the fruit bowl on the kitchen table he chose an apple. He put the food and the morning paper into the basket, on top of the towel. He went upstairs once more to fetch a tartan travelling rug, his linen jacket and an old panama hat. He was ready.

Mr Catterick locked the front door, turning the key twice, and set off for the station. It was a hot June day, with a few clouds streaking the intense blue of the sky. In a brief moment of doubt Mr Catterick had worried that it might rain or be overcast on his birthday. He remembered how it had always seemed important that the weather was fine for his birthday when he was a child. The man on the radio had said that the heatwave was likely to last for another week. Mr Catterick imagined that there might be a lot of people at Brighton on a hot Saturday in June, and he looked forward to jostling amongst the crowd.

At the ticket office Mr Catterick asked for a second class day return to Brighton.

'Have you got your rail card?' asked a sullen British Rail employee.

'I wasn't aware that I had to have a card,' said Mr Catterick.

'Your senior citizen rail card,' explain the man impatiently.

'I am not a senior citizen,' said Mr Catterick. 'I am a beautiful old man.'

Mr Catterick declined the offer of help from a gangling youth, and heaved his basket onto the luggage rack. He had been shocked by the price of the ticket, since he rarely travelled by rail, but he was determined that nothing should spoil the day. He took off his panama hat, placing it on the seat beside him, and began to read his newspaper as the train pulled out of the station. The news was uninteresting, seemingly remote, even though one of the main items concerned a debate in parliament about pensions. Mr Catterick read the obituary of an actress who had died in relative obscurity at the age of sixty-eight. He learned that she had been a great beauty in her time, by which the obituarist had meant her youth, and a rather blurred photograph at the head of the column seemed to confirm this. Mr Catterick remembered seeing her once in a production of *As You Like It*. Sitting in the darkened auditorium, he had sensed once more the unmistakable thrill of the theatre. Perhaps, had he become an actor rather than a solicitor, he might have acted opposite this actress, declaring love for her in the words of a great writer. But there would be no regrets today.

Mr Catterick left the station and made his way down a wide street towards the front, passing antique shops, cafés, churches, a cinema, amusement arcades and a shop selling all kinds of rock, including some in the shape of dentures. When he reached the front and saw the shingle and beyond it the sea, through peppermint-painted, iron railings, he turned left and walked along past piles of deck-chairs, information kiosks and ice-cream stalls. He scanned the shore, but saw only family groups, lying in the sun, or splashing along the water's edge. Small dots that were people's heads bobbed amongst the waves, and cries of laughter and fear rang out clearly in the still noon air. Mr Catterick continued walking, then went down a flight of steps onto a lower level, amongst fairground machines and past empty coaches, their drivers lying back in their seats dozing. It was a longer walk than Mr Catterick had imagined. He padded along silently like an old labrador, looking from left to right. A small railway track ran alongside him, and in the distance he saw a small engine and carriages, painted yellow and brown, moving slowly. Ahead there seemed to be a sudden density of people, and to his left, rising steeply, was a long bank covered in rhododendrons, their naturally dark and glossy leaves dulled by dust.

As he approached, Mr Catterick became aware that for such

a large crowd of people there was very little noise. He waited for the engine and carriages, loaded with children, to pass before crossing the railway line onto the shingle. The smooth irregular-shaped pebbles crunched and shifted under his feet. Looking back towards the mound he saw a row of people along the railings; the bright sunlight glinted on a pair of binoculars. There was a ledge along the strand where the shingle dropped away to a lower level, so that Mr Catterick could not immediately see the object of everyone's attention, although he knew what it was.

'Excuse me,' said Mr Catterick, easing through the murmuring crowd.

'I don't think you'd better look, grandad,' said a man wearing stained beige slacks and an olive, nylon sports-shirt. Several people laughed.

'I'm not a grandfather, actually,' said Mr Catterick. 'And I have not come to *look*. Now, if you'll excuse me. . .'

'I'll bet! Dirty old man!' And more people laughed. Mr Catterick ignored them and moved forward. He could now see the handful of naked people, lying on the shingle alone and in groups, with ill-feigned nonchalance. One couple was sitting up, backs to the crowd, talking quietly and awkwardly. A further group of young people, bodies glistening, splashed and shouted in the sea like children. None of the sunbathers was over forty. Mr Catterick noticed that most of them were bronzed; two men sporting moustaches and neat, short hair were a particularly rich shade of mahogany, their silken bodies sparkling with oil. I am pale, but comely, thought Mr Catterick as he put down his basket, and laid out his rug.

Mr Catterick remembered the school play as he took off his hat and jacket, and laid them neatly on the rug. The storm had been poorly simulated, for the school had not equipped the hall with a sophisticated lighting rig. Small boys had squeaked farewell to wives and children as the school percussionists improvised in the wings. 'Good luck,' J. R. Smethwick had whispered, looking up at Catterick, his painted lips stretching in a wide grin. Catterick had adjusted his magician's robes, lately the masters' common room curtains, and smiled back at the junior. Mr Catterick felt the same tense anticipation now, as he removed his tie and began unbuttoning his shirt. Concentrate upon the cue; try to relax; here it comes, Smethwick's kohl-lined eyes wide with concern:

> Had I been any god of power, I would
> Have sunk the sea within the earth, or ere
> It should the good ship so have swallowed and
> The fraughting souls within her.
>
> Be collected.
> No more amazement.

– and it had started. Catterick knew that the audience had included both friends and enemies, but as the words began, he no longer thought of them, but of the old man on his island.

As Mr Catterick unzipped his trousers he noticed out of the corner of his eye the two mahogany men looking at him with alarm, their sunglasses raised.

'He's not really going to?' said one with undisguised distaste.

'I'm afraid he is,' replied the other languidly. Mr Catterick felt a momentary disgust for the arrogance of youth, with its self-assured narcissism. He folded his trousers meticulously, feeling suddenly vulnerable in his underpants. It was not the same, of course, not at all. Here there was no disguising greasepaint and none of the camouflage of assumed costume and character. This, for all the world to see, was Edgar Charles Mahew Catterick, widower, aged seventy-one this very day. Mr Catterick emerged from his underpants, which had been clean on this morning. He was facing the crowd, calm and serene. Naked came I out of my mother's womb, and naked shall I return thither, thought Mr Catterick. But not yet; not, indeed, for some time. He sat down gingerly on the rug, feeling the stones beneath pressing the weave of the material into his skin. He had to admit that it was really most uncomfortable. He lay back exposing himself fully to the sun, feeling its intensity almost as a weight. Through eyes narrowed against the light, Mr Catterick looked down the length of his body, over his raised ribcage and flattened belly to the almost white, downy hair where his privates nestled. In the distance were his strong, white feet, slightly splayed, the joints of the toes large and sprouting coarse hair. And beyond was the sea, glassy but mobile, with the shimmering forms of bathers leaping and bobbing amidst the waves.

Mr Catterick, painfully aware of the stones beneath his shoulders and buttocks, decided to stroll down to the sea. He picked up his towel and checking the natural gesture of wrapping it around his waist, draped it over one arm. He took his hat and put it on his head. It probably looked ridiculous, but at seventy-one one did need some protection from the sun.

He was without props, without the bright carapace of youth, the chrysalis of his former life shed. With awkward movements he made his way across the shingle towards the irridescent water, a lone figure, slightly stooped, rather scrawny, naked except for a panama hat.

Setting the World Aright
John Haylock

Jim Spenser, unmarried, fifty-seven, retired from a City bank, had chosen to live in the South East Asian republic as it was one of the cheapest countries in the world, and no income tax was levied on foreign residents whose incomes derived from abroad. He settled into a furnished flat in a large apartment block in the capital's tourist district, a quarter of hotels, airline offices, restaurants, hostess bars, gay bars and curio shops. The quarter was bordered by a grand boulevard that skirted the bay, over which the sun set magnificently, and a congested avenue that ran out to a suburb. Jim took up residence in this quarter because it seemed convenient; in the vicinity was a club, once only for Americans but now open to those natives who could pay the substantial entrance fee and annual subscription. The club's main asset was a swimming pool up and down which Jim swam each afternoon.

Jim had never been particularly sociable and so he did not mind spending most of the day alone. He had taken up the two introductions a friend in London had given him, and the friends (one English, the other American) of his friend had behaved punctiliously, inviting him to dinner and putting him up for the club. But Jim had not returned their hospitality. He disliked entertaining, was no good at it, and he was not a very congenial guest. He would pass the time of day with these new acquaintances at the club and sometimes sit with a glass of beer, which he bought at the bar, at their lunch table, never eating himself – he preferred snacks in his room. Sometimes the conversation would turn to the subject of corruption, which the friends said was rife in the country.

'I haven't noticed any corruption,' remarked the innocent Jim.

'You're not in business,' replied one of the friends of the London friend, bitterly.

Jim planned his week as methodically as if he were in business; instead of a series of appointments and meetings he had a programme of visits to the shops, to the bank, to the post office and so on. Monday was 'bread' day, Tuesday 'bank' day, Wednesday 'letter-writing and post-office' day, Thursday 'supermarket' day, Friday 'laundry' day (he prided himself on his ironing) and as in his City days Saturdays and Sundays were days off. These duties were matutinal ones. The afternoons were devoted to a siesta followed by a swim – twelve lengths of the thirty-metre pool. On each evening at seven his appointment with the BBC World Service fell due, and this coincided with 'rum' time – rum and lime, both local products and therefore cheap, had become his favourite tipple. And then there was supper prepared more often than not through a 'rum' haze. He would forget ingredients and boil cabbage without salt and eat a pork chop without gravy or apple sauce; once he tried to cook an omelette with no fat in the pan. However, he put up with his amateur culinary efforts.

Jim was content, more so than at any time in his life. He had hated his work in the bank, the dreary English climate, the monotonous existence of convention that he had led with his mother in Kensington. As soon as she had died he resigned and took off on his own (he was an only child and had no close relations) not to any of the obvious places like Spain or Malta or Cyprus, but to the South East Asian country which had always drawn him because it was about as far as one could get from Britain. As a child he had put one finger on England and another on the other side of the globe and said, 'I want to go there,' and now he was 'there', really 'there'. At times he could hardly believe it. It was wonderful to be in a land where it was always warm and not ever to have to wear a dark suit and tie and to be able to go about in nothing but a short-sleeved shirt, summer slacks and rubber sandals. Being a tyro unused to the expatriate scene Jim expected things and people to be much the same as they were at home; he was surprised and even indig-

nant when he found they weren't. Of course he realized that
the people were poor, although summer clothing, shirt and
trousers or a simple dress disguised their poverty, and he knew
that salaries were low and accommodation often wretched,
but this was the East.

Jim became impatient about the slow delivery of letters.
Why should letters take weeks to reach him from Europe
when planes flew there in under twenty-four hours? He asked
the porter in the office of his apartments but the young man
only smiled a generous smile and said he didn't know. Jim's
club friends explained that it was due to inefficiency and the
general idleness that gripped the country.

'Give the postman or the sorter a tip and you'll get your
letters in proper time,' one of them said.

Jim, though, found bribery odious.

'Why,' he asked, 'should I pay extra for my letters? The
postal charges are arranged by international agreement and
are reciprocal and are meant to include delivery. In England
we don't have to tip the postman.'

'You're not in England,' came the riposte.

'I know I'm not,' returned Jim, peevishly.

Stung by the club acquaintance's retort Jim decided to call at
the General Post Office and complain. The building was not
far away and could be reached by first walking through a park
and then crossing two busy thoroughfares. He had learnt how
to negotiate the unruly traffic and knew when it was the
moment to stand still in the middle of a wide bustling street
and when he should scurry. He scurried across the road on the
other side of which stood the GPO, a grandiose, pseudo-
Greek edifice, yellow in colour, with porticos, pediments and
Corinthian pillars. Up the steps he trudged, sweating a bit,
and he entered the lofty main hall, where people were queue-
ing at selling windows protected by iron mesh. At a window
labelled 'Information' he asked a pretty, buxom girl with a
mass of black hair and a snub nose whom he should see about
postal delivery. He was directed to an office containing several
tables behind which officials in khaki uniforms sat, talked,

smoked or read. Jim approached the nearest table and inquired of an official who was engrossed in a book of comics if he could see whoever was in charge of postal delivery to his quarter of the capital. 'My letters take a very long time to get to me,' Jim complained. The official, a portly man with sleek, dark hair, deigned to abandon his reading assignment for a moment and flicked his eyes up at Jim, not failing, Jim felt, to notice his casual outfit.

'Fill up this form.' The official pushed a buff-coloured piece of paper towards Jim and then returned to his book. After completing the form, Jim placed it in front of the official, who read with the help of a finger a few more captions before he initialled it with a flourish and shoved it back across the table again. More than an hour of waiting and seeing other officials passed before Jim finally gained the presence of a senior official, a director, possibly, who had a carpeted and air-cooled office of his own. This official, unlike the more junior ones, was, perhaps because he was sure, or less uncertain, of his position, polite and pleasant.

'Where are you living?' asked the official.

Jim gave the name of his apartment building, wondering if its reputation were notorious.

'That is in the tourist section, an expensive quarter.' The director's English had the same lilt to it as the language of the country; although he spoke correctly he was not always easy to understand; his stresses were inclined to fall on the final syllables of words.

'So you think your let-*ters* are delay-*ed?*'

'I don't see why it should take three weeks for air mail to get here.'

The official put the tips of his fingers together carefully, slowly, pad to pad, the little fingers first.

'There is the busi-*ness* of the sor-*ting*. And our post-*men* are paid very little. I will tell you the truth, Mr Spen-*ser*. Our post-*men* only get two dol-*lars* a day, and they have to pay for their own transport; so they cannot come to work every day.'

'D'you mean to say that your *post*-men don't work every day?'

'It may cost them half a day's salary to get to their post off-*ice*.'

'What about the sorters?'

'The sor-*ters* do not deli-*ver*.'

'I didn't imagine that they did,' said Jim, impatiently. 'But couldn't they be quicker with their sorting?'

'They are paid by the hour so for them to be quick means less pay.'

Jim sighed. 'Can nothing be done?'

'You could help your post-*man*. That is up to you, of course, but you could help him.'

'Help him? How could I help him? You mean with his deliveries?'

The director smiled.

'You mean give him a – ' Jim, not liking to breathe the distasteful word 'bribe', didn't finish his sentence.

The director's smile did not alter; it remained fixed and broad while Jim left his room.

'I really think,' said Jim the next day to one of his club acquaintances, 'that the director meant that I should bribe the postman to bring my letters more quickly.'

'Of course he did.'

'But it's monstrous.'

'You should have a post office box and collect your own mail.'

'That's such a nuisance. I'll write to the *Courier*.'

'It won't do any good.'

The acquaintance was right. Jim sent a letter to Max Pinay, a journalist who had a weekly column entitled 'Complain to Me'. The column was based on a reader's letter of complaint about some aspect or another: high prices in a supermarket; circuitous bus routes; the inconvenience of certain one-way streets; the siting of the folk-art village. Postal delivery, however, did not seem important enough to be taken up for all Jim got was a courteous acknowledgement.

'The Post Office is a Government Department,' explained the acquaintance. 'You can't expect a semi-government newspaper to criticize the Government.'

'How was I to know?'

'Everyone knows.'

'You might have told me.'

Jim liked his Monday chore, that of walking a sweaty mile down a street polluted by exhaust fumes to Rita's bakery. No early riser since the glorious days of retirement had begun, towards eleven o'clock Jim sauntered along the pavement of Miguel Pacifico Street, a narrow, one-way thoroughfare that ran parallel to the great seaside avenue. The street was closely packed with cars, buses, motor-cycles and small covered trucks converted into passenger transporters that moved slowly and jerkily as if on a hesitant production belt. Jim liked to go this way to Rita's because it pleased him that the seedy men who lolled outside souvenir shops, offering a slightly higher rate for the dollar than the official one, did not accost him, nor was he pestered by the shoeblacks or the pedlars of imitation precious stones; and the blousy girls who sat by the doors of go-go bars did not so much as throw him a glance. Being ignored by these mongers made him feel that he belonged, though his shock of white hair, his ruddy, clean-shaven face and his cornflower-blue eyes made him stand out from the natives, who were predominantly brown-skinned, black-haired and black-eyed.

Rita's bakery was down a side street near a grey stone church with a red tin roof and next to a dressmaker's named 'Mary's Fashions'. Jim turned off Miguel Pacifico and approached Rita's. He liked the enormous Rita. She was so cheerful and always ready for a chat. He thought she liked him too. Today, however, contrary to his expectation, she was not her usual vivacious self; instead, she was gloomy, cast down.

'What's the matter?'

'There was a fire up the street,' she explained. 'The firemen they come and they cut off the electrici-*tee*; they put out the fire, yes; not big fire. Did they put back the electrici-*tee*? No. They say they cannot. That is job for electrici-*tee* company. We must wait. I can't wait. I need electrici-*tee* for my work, my o-*ven*. We ask electric company to come. A man come, yes, he come, but without pay from us he will not put back electric power. He want one thousand from each shop. What have we done? Why should we pay one thousand? We did not make the fire. We did not cut off the electrici-*tee*. Why we pay one thou-*sand*?'

'Did you pay a thousand?' Jim had made a rough calculation; a thousand was about one hundred dollars, which was probably a lot for Rita.

'Yes, of course we pay. How we not pay? If we no pay I have no work. I cannot bake, Mr Spen-*ser*.'

'You should have refused.'

'How we refuse? The man he say if you no pay, no electrici-*tee*. What I do, Mr Spen-*ser*?'

'I will see what I can do,' said Jim. 'Maybe I can get your thousand back.'

'You can?'

'Maybe.'

'You are very kind.' She handed Jim his loaf, still warm it was. 'How you get it back?' she asked challengingly as she gave him his change; her dark eyes dipped into his blue ones for a moment.

'I'll see what I can do.'

'I no work for three days because the electrici-*tee* is off. First time it happen. First time this shop shut since I o-*pen*. I just shut one day in the year, Holy Friday; you know that Mr Spen-*ser*. I work on Christ-*mas*. Last week, I shut three days. I lose money and must pay one thou-*sand*.'

On his way home Jim composed a letter to Max Pinay of the *Courier*, and as soon as he got to his apartment he sat down and wrote it. 'I should like to draw your attention to a gross injustice which has come to my notice. . .' He did not mention Rita's name but he did give the name of her street. When he told one of his club acquaintances what he had done, the acquaintance, an American businessman of many years' standing in the country, said, 'It's just a waste of time to try and interfere with the way things are run here.'

'I hate unfairness, especially when it's meted out to the poor.'

'The poor always get kicked around. They expect it.'

'You'll say they enjoy their lot next.' Jim was roused; his uneasiness about the effect of the letter put him on the defensive too. 'I feel I must help Rita. She works so hard.'

'I don't suppose she'll miss the hundred dollars.'

'That's not the point,' said Jim, irritably. 'She should never have had to pay a bribe in order to get her current switched back on. It's the kind of thing that makes me writhe, this squeezing money out of people.'

'It's the system here. Salaries are low and have to be supplemented.'

'Is the electric light company a private concern?'

'Yes.'

'Then perhaps Max Pinay will take up the case.'

In the following day's issue of the *Courier* the columnist devoted all his space to an attack on the employees of the electric light company for extorting bribes from the shop-keepers in Rita's street. 'Shame on us,' the article concluded, 'that it has taken a foreigner to lay bare such an iniquity. Mr James Spenser, who is British, has lived among us for only six months. We should be grateful to him.'

A twinge of pride and pleasure ran through Jim when he read the 'Complain to me' column in the *Courier*. It was the first time he had seen his name in print in a newspaper. At the club, though, his acquaintances were far from pleased.

'You don't think you've helped any, do you?' said one.

'They'll take it out on Rita,' said another, 'if not on you.'

'I did not give her name. What could they do to me?'

The next morning the telephone rang in Jim's flat, an unusual occurrence.

'Hello?' he said, timidly. 'Am I speaking to Mr Spenser?' The accent was strongly American.

'Yes.'

'This is Max Pinay. I'm truly grateful to you, Mr Spenser, for your valuable information. This is a great case. The President may be interested. He's all against corruption. I need more details. Could you come and see me?'

Jim went. Although Mr Pinay had an American accent and could have been a national of heterogeneous USA, he was in fact a native who had been educated in California. He was older than his voice had suggested; grey and fat, yet smooth with a cunning regard. His office was plush. He sprang out of his chair as Jim entered.

'Ah, Mr Spenser, the conscience of our soul. We are truly grateful, truly. Please sit down.'

Jim sat on the other side of the wide, polished desk.

'Cigarette, Mr Spenser?'

'No, thank you.'

'Now, Mr Spenser, we need more details in order to properly investigate this affair.'

'Yes?' said Jim, uncertainly.

'We need to know the name or names of the person or persons who told you that he or she or they had to bribe the electric company mechanics to reconnect the current. Without the name or names we can't do much.'

'I'm afraid it's impossible for me to give the name without asking them first.'

'Is that so? If you told me who told you then – '

'No, I'm sorry.'

'If I came with you.'

Jim shook his head.

'Then – ' Mr Pinay threw his hands into the air. 'You want to help these people, right?'

'Yes,' replied Jim, who was beginning to wish he had not written to the *Courier*.

'Then. . .' the journalist's hands went up into the air again.

Jim sighed. 'I'll tell you what I'll do –'

'Yes?' said Mr Pinay, sharply.

'I'll ask them myself if I may reveal their names, and if they agree I'll tell you.'

'Okay, Mr Spenser.'

Jim's morning routine was too fixed a one for him to cut short any of the procedures – shaving, showering, boiling an egg, making a piece of toast, listening to the news and reading the newspaper – so it was not until after eleven the next day that he strolled down Miguel Pacifico towards Rita's bakery; the fact that he was looking forward to telling Rita what he'd done on her behalf did not make him hurry. 'She'll be so pleased,' Jim told himself, but when he told her she was far from pleased.

'Oh, I do wish you had not done it,' she said.

'But why? We may get your money back. We'll shame the company into giving you your money back. Now, may I tell them your name?'

'No, please, no.' Rita seemed really alarmed.

'But I want to help.'

'Oh, I do wish you had not done it, Mr Spen-*ser*.'

'Don't you see that if you submit to such a demand and pay up, pay the company man money he's no right to have, then the whole corrupt system will never end. Your admitting to paying the money will help the country, set an example. So may I give the newspaper your name?'

'No, please, no.'

Rita was adamant and Jim had to inform the columnist that he could not reveal the name. Mr Pinay told him that this would weaken the case against the company. 'You cannot accuse without evidence, Mr Spenser.'

The next day was 'supermarket' day and Jim, armed with his plastic shopping bag, descended from his seventh floor apartment at his usual hour of eleven. As he passed the office, the young porter said, 'Man to see you, sir.'

A man of about thirty, tidily dressed in shirt and trousers, came forward. 'Mr Spenser, sir?'

'Yes.' The man explained that he was from the electric light company and asked if Jim would go with him to the head office as the directors wanted to have more details about the alleged extortion. 'We are grateful to you for reporting this affair, this bad affair,' the man said. 'We want your help more.' Jim agreed to accompany the man to the headquarters of the firm, which they reached after a shortish drive in an air-conditioned, chauffeur-driven Mercedes. In what seemed like a board room Jim was introduced to a number of company executives, some in dark suits, others in embroidered, white shirts with frog fastenings that hung outside their navy-blue trousers. When Jim had shaken hands all round and had received searching looks (he was in his customary casual clothes and rubber sandals) he was invited to sit at the table. When he had done so, a middle-aged, blue-suited man began to speak.

'We are very pleased you brought up this matter, Mr Spen-*ser*,' he said. 'We are very anxious to punish the offenders. We cannot do so unless we know the names of those who say they were asked to pay the money. We have made enquiries and none of the shop people in the street say they had to pay for having their current turned back on after the fire.'

'They are lying.'

The chairman or whatever he was rose, 'Will you come with us, Mr Spen-*ser*, to the street and we will ask the shop-keepers.'

'No, I cannot. I promised not to tell the name.'

'You say name, not names. There was only one who told you he had to pay?' One of the other directors tried to press Jim, but to no avail, he would not budge, and the meeting ended, albeit with apparent cordiality, though the Mercedes was not summoned to drive him home.

For the second day running Jim's routine was broken and instead of going to the supermarket he went to Rita's bakery. 'Did a man from the electric light company come and see you?'

'Yes,' she answered, 'he come and he ask me if I pay anyone to have the power put on again after the fire.'

'And what did yout tell him?'

'I tell him we no pay.'

'But you *did* pay.'

'Yes, we pay but we say we no pay. We cannot say – '

'But you should tell the truth; if you told the truth you'd get your money back.'

'If we say we pay, it bad for us maybe.' Rita looked down.

'But the law would protect you.'

'You don't understand this coun-*tree*, Mr Spen-*ser*.'

At the club they agreed with Rita. 'You can't try and put the world right here,' a club acquaintance told Jim. 'It's best to let things as they are.'

With a wounded, yet at the same time defiant look in his blue eyes, Jim said, 'I did what I thought was right. If someone doesn't try and do something then – '

His sentence was cut off by laughter.

A few days later when Jim came in from visiting the foreign bank in which he kept a current account (it was a 'bank' day) he switched on the light in the hall of his apartment and it didn't work. 'The bulb, I suppose. Hell!' Jim was weary as the bank was some distance off in a business section of the spread-out city which took an hour to reach in a 'truck' bus, the cheapest form of transport available. Jim never took a taxi. Because of the heavy midday traffic it had taken over an hour and a half of sitting among other passengers, sweating, inhaling exhaust fumes and having his ears punished by the taped 'pop' music the drivers of these little private buses played as an attraction. Jim was tired, hungry and fractious. He tried the bedroom light and then the sitting room one and they didn't work either. He opened the refrigerator door and no little welcoming beam came on; the air-cooler was silent. 'The electricity must have failed. A 'brown' out. Damn! But the lift worked.' He rang down to the porter's office and was told that there had been no power failure. He ate a sandwich and drank a warm rum and lime and then asked the office again but no explanation was forthcoming. Exhausted and furious, he lay on his bed, but could not sleep; it was so hot. He got up and rang the office again. The porter told him that the electricity had perhaps been cut off through the non-payment of his bill. 'But I've paid my bill,' stormed Jim.

'I'll call the company,' said the porter.

Three frustrating days without light, cooling, ice or cooking, as his electric stove wouldn't work, reduced Jim's morale to a low ebb. Several calls to the electric light company only brought polite promises. On the fourth day when Jim was becoming quite desperate due to the discomfort and inconvenience caused by the lack of electricity a man from the company came to see him. 'We are very sorry, Mr Spen-*ser*, but we cannot do anything until you pay your deposit.'

'What deposit?' Jim had not allowed the official over the threshold.

'The deposit everyone must pay when he move into an apartment.'

'I was not told about this.'

'The management of the apartment company make a mistake. We are very sorry, but we cannot reconnect until you pay the deposit you should have paid when you move in.'

'I refuse to pay.'

'Then we cannot connect.' The electric company official, a balding, thin, brown man with black-rimmed spectacles in front of his dark eyes produced a book of regulations and showed Jim a paragraph that said a new tenant must lodge a deposit. 'Why wasn't I told?' asked Jim.

'It is the mistake of the management.'

'How much is the deposit?'

'A thousand – '

'A hundred dollars?'

'Yes.'

'And if I don't pay?'

'You will not be reconnected, I regret to say.'

Later that day when he ran into one of his club acquaintances he made no mention of the incident.

One of a Kind

Julian Barnes

I always had this theory about Romania. Well, not a proper theory; more an observation, I suppose. Have you ever realized how, in various fields, Romania has managed to produce one – but only one – significant artist? It's as if the race only has enough strength for one of anything – like those plants which channel all their energy into a single bloom. So: one great sculptor – Brancusi; one playwright – Ionesco; one composer – Enuscu; one cartoonist – Steinberg. Even one great popular myth – Dracula.

I once mentioned this theory at a literary party to a Romanian writer in exile. Marian Tiriac was a sallow, plump, combative man, and I had got off on the wrong foot with him by referring to the question of 'dissidents'. It's always an awkward word to use with Eastern European exiles, as I should have realized. Some of them take the high political line of 'It is the Government who are the dissidents'; others the personal, practical one of 'I am not a dissident; I am a writer.' I had idly asked Tiriac whether there were any dissidents in Romania. He swished the remnants of some publisher's white wine round in the bottom of his glass, as aggressively as he could without losing any of it, and replied:

'There are no dissidents in Romania. There are merely a few people who are unavailable for comment to the foreign press. In any case, they live some way from Bucharest. The roads aren't too good up near the Hungarian border; nor are your journalists very inquisitive.'

He said it with irony, but also with a sort of funny pride, as if I didn't have the right to an opinion – or even a question – on the subject of his homeland. Not wishing to give in, but also not wishing to irritate him further, I then brought up my Romanian Theory; which I did with due English meekness and hesitancy and pleading of ignorance. Tiriac smiled at me genially enough, and reached for another stuffed olive.

'You forget poetry,' he said. 'Eminescu.' It was a name I had vaguely encountered, so I gave a nod of disgraced recognition. 'And tennis – Nastase.' Another nod; was he sending me up? 'And party leadership – Ceausescu.' Now he was.

'What about novelists?' I persisted. 'Is there one I should have heard of?'

'No,' he replied, with a doleful shake of the head. 'There are none. We have no novelists.'

I forgot this conversation for almost a year, when I was invited to attend a conference of young writers in Bucharest. The occasion was as pleasant as it was pointless – I listened to dozens of vague if well-intentioned speeches about the duty of the writer towards mankind, and about the power of the written word to shape men's souls – but at least it got me to a country I wouldn't otherwise have visited. There were banquets with plum brandy, and an excursion to the Danube delta where we strained our eyes for distant flights of pelican, and parties at which local officials asked you serious questions about the craft of writing – questions which made you feel slightly ashamed, as if you ought to take your vocation more earnestly than you did.

The last morning of the trip was designated free time, and I strolled round the city with an Italian writer of experimental verse. We looked into small, dark churches, silent except for the crackling of beeswax candles and the shuffling of old people. We visited the Art Museum of the Socialist Republic of Romania, where we saw a Van Eyck portrait of an olive-skinned burgher in a blue headdress; the nameplate had been worn away by reverent fingers, as if this, the finest painting in the gallery, had become an icon to be touched no less usefully than the sculpted feet of Mary. Finally, we strolled along the Calea Victoriei and looked into the shops. On a corner of the Palatul Republicii, opposite the Headquarters of the Central

Committee, we found a bookshop. One of the windows was devoted to a single work, a novel by someone called Nicolai Petrescu; we stared at the pyramid of copies for a while, wondering if we had met the author in the previous seven days. A small photograph at the corner of the display – showing a plump, white-bearded man with rimless spectacles – confirmed that we hadn't. Since this appeared to be one of the main bookshops in the country, and Petrescu, presumably, one of its more important writers, it struck us as slightly odd that he hadn't been wheeled out for some free plum brandy along with all the others.

My companion and I looked briefly into the Western languages section of the shop – if you're foreign, it's best to be dead as well if you plan to sell in Bucharest – and moved on. Later that day we were driven to Otopeni airport and flew home.

I didn't see Marian Tiriac for some months afterwards, but when I did I offered to give him my impressions of the country he hadn't seen in thirty years of exile. He seemed discouragingly unexcited by the idea, and informed me that since he would certainly never return, he made a point of not finding out what had become of the place. During his first few years of exile, he had been bitter and nostalgic, and had kept up a plaintive correspondence with many friends; but this had made things worse rather than better, and he had now severed all contact.

'Well, in any case,' I went on. 'You weren't telling me the truth. There *are* novelists in Romania.'

'Oh, perhaps. You mean Rebreanu. Or maybe Sadoveanu. I'm afraid they're only thesis material nowadays. They are not the Brancusi and Nastase you seek.'

'No, I wasn't saying that.' I hardly could have been, since I hadn't recognized either of the names. 'I just meant there were a few around. A few we met.' I mentioned three or four. He shook his head.

'You must remember, I do not have much interest in these things nowadays.'

'And there was someone else – we saw a lot of copies of something of his in a window. Petrescu; Nicolai Petrescu.'

'Ah,' he said sharply. 'Ah. Nicolai; you saw Nicolai. They are still selling his book? And how is he?'

I explained that we hadn't actually met him. I described the bookshop in Calea Victoriei, the window display, and the small picture in the corner. I said that as far as one could tell from a photo, the writer seemed to be well.

'And did he have anything in his buttonhole? A little decoration of some sort?'

'You mean a flower?'

'Of course not. A decoration. A badge.'

I said I couldn't remember. Tiriac settled himself further down into the sofa, and balanced his glass on the arm.

'I will tell you about Nicolai Petrescu if you like.' I did like. 'But you must not necessarily believe everything I say because I knew him very well. You must – what is that expression in shooting? – you must aim off. You must aim off for truth, I think.

'Nicolai and I are about the same age – our middle fifties. We were both just young enough to miss the war, for which we used to give many thanks. Fighting for the Germans against the Russians, and then changing ends and fighting for the Russians against the Germans was not particularly pleasant by all accounts. The bullets could come from either direction, or even both at the same time. But we missed much of that, fortunately.

'We were about eighteen or so when what the present administration likes to refer to as "the national anti-fascist and anti-imperialist insurrection" took place. Two men and a dog and a home-made flag, plus the fraternal Russian army – that's what that means. The Russians came in, drove out the Germans, and looked around for the local Communists. The only trouble was, they couldn't find any. Do you know how big the Communist party was in Romania in 1944? Two football teams. So, the Russians stayed around for a bit, helping to build socialism – or at least party membership – until they thought it was more or less safe to go. They sort of went in 1947. Sort of.

'Nicolai and I were at polytechnic together at that time. We were – how shall I put it? – good middle-class boys. We weren't fascists or anything; we just weren't from the working class. What's more, we both wanted to be writers. You see the problem?'

I nodded. I thought how much better he had aged than Petrescu. Tiriac looked to be in his mid-forties; Petrescu could have been over sixty from his photo.

'I suppose, when it comes down to it, it's a question of temperament more than talent, which way a writer goes. In that sort of place, anyway. We talked about it a lot. Not when we went along to the Writers' Union, of course; but between the two of us. I'm – well, you could say I was idealistic if you wanted to, but maybe it's just that I'm despairing by temperament. I only thought of the difficulties; I only thought of what they wouldn't let you write, not of what they would. I took a rather hard line on everything in those days: I believed – well, perhaps I still do – that if you can't write exactly what you want to, then you shouldn't write anything. Silence, or exile, you could say. Well, I chose exile. I lost my language, and half my talent. So I still have a lot to be despairing about.

'Nicolai, well, he was of a different temperament. No – not a collaborator at all. He was a nice man; he was my friend. He was very intelligent, I remember, and just as despairing as me, but somehow more cynical in his mind. Perhaps I don't mean cynical – perhaps I just mean he had a sense of humour. I chose silence and exile; he chose cunning.

'You know what they call wedding-cake architecture?' I nodded. I'd seen quite enough of it on my few brief trips to Eastern Europe. 'Well, the very worst examples you can see – outside Russia, I mean – the biggest, the nastiest, the ones in the most overpowering positions in the cities, are the ones which were imposed by Stalin. Gifts of the Soviet people, they were called, to Warsaw, or wherever. Monstrosities they are. People walk past on the opposite side of the road and have a quiet spit just when they come level with them. The street-cleaners are more busy opposite these wedding-cake monstrosities than anywhere else in the whole city.

'Nicolai one day conceived this plan to write what he called the wedding-cake novel. We'd been at a particularly foul and depressing meeting of the Writers' Union, and went for a walk afterwards in Cismigiu park, and I remember Nicolai turning to me as we reached the edge of the lake and saying, "If that's what they want, then that is what I shall give them." I might have pushed him in the lake, except that I saw he was smiling at me, very broadly. And then he began to explain his idea.

'The wedding-cake novel was also to be a sort of Trojan horse. Leave it outside the city and let them wheel it in; that way they'll be even more pleased. So Nicolai started working on his book. It was, of course, an epic: epically historical, epically sentimental, epically improving, epically realistic. And at the same time he began to speak at meetings of the Writers' Union. "I have this problem, comrades . . ." he would begin, and he would refer to his novel, and explain some difficulty he had come across – the problem of realistically conveying the point of view of fascist anti–patriots, for instance, or the question of handling sexual experience without offending the intrinsic good taste of the bookbuying steel–worker of Ploesti. That sort of thing. He would act troubled, and then slowly allow the clodheads and buffoons of the Union to guide him into their way of thinking, to lead him towards the light. "I have this problem, comrades . . ." Every time I heard him say it, I thought, They'll see through him this time, surely. But then irony is not a mode with which the committee were too familiar.

'And so Nicolai continued with his book, and by suggesting all these problems he was having with it, managed to create within the Union a certain apprehension. You can imagine how it is – they don't want anyone to rock the boat. If one writer steps out of line, it places everyone else in jeopardy. Nicolai was very good at playing on this fear, and the fact that he never brought any of his book along to read worried them a bit too. He kept saying that he needed to do another draft to correct a few final errors. "I have this problem, comrades . . ."

'He showed me bits of it, though he had to be careful, because I was getting into disfavour by now. Too despairing, they said of me. The few scraps of work I offered to publish were held to be insufficiently uplifting to the human spirit. Uplifting . . . ha. As if writing were a brassière and the human spirit were a pair of bosoms.

'Nicolai was a very good writer. The parts he let me see were wonderful. I mean, they were entirely awful as well, but they were wonderful too. They weren't satirical – he didn't want to do it that way. What he did was to put on a false heart and then write from the bottom of it. This false heart was intensely patriotic, sentimental and documentary. There was a lot about how little food people had, and much reference to Romanian history and the sturdiness of the national character. The history, of course, had to be vetted by the Union. "Comrades – I have another little problem . . ." I can see him now.'

Tiriac gave a chuckle as he thought of his friend, a sad chuckle. I could see how easily he appeared despairing, even when he was amused.

'And then?'

'And then he finished it, and he called it, naturally, *The Wedding Cake*. He couldn't resist the title, and he put in a long passage of facile symbolism about a wedding cake, just to back it up. He wanted the book to be like one of Stalin's presents to his slave nations. He wanted it to stand there, grand and half-admired at first, but always unignorable. And then gradually, just by standing there, it would begin to make people wonder about it. And the longer it stood there and the more it had been praised, the more it would end by shaming and embarrassing those who had revered it.

'I asked him what he would do after it was published; if his plan worked. "I shall do nothing," he said. "I shan't write another word. That will make the joke clearer as the years go by." "But they might try and make you," I said to him, "they don't let people not work, you know." "Well, maybe I'll be too famous by then. Besides, I shall tell them I have put all my heart and all my soul into *The Wedding Cake*. 'If you want to read a second book by me,' I shall say, 'Read the first one again.' And then I shall sit back and try and look as distinguished as possible.''

'I left the country in 1951, when Nicolai still had some way to go with his book; he had about thirty-five strands of narrative, and they all had to be tied off in neat granny knots. We never wrote to one another after I left, because it would have been difficult for him. Instead I wrote to . . . unimportant people. My mother, a few harmless friends. As you know, I haven't ever been back; I haven't heard any news for almost a quarter of a century. But in one of her last letters to me before she died, my mother told me that *The Wedding Cake* had been published with enormous success. She had not read the book – her eyesight was poor and she didn't want to make it worse – but she wrote and told me about it. "And to think," she said, "If you had stayed, my Marian, you might have been the success that Nicolai now is." ' '

He turned back towards me, and took another swig of wine. He seemed depressed by his story. Then he smiled.

'Actually, if I'd known, I'd have got you to bring me a copy of *The Wedding Cake*,' he said. 'It might have been – what? – good for a laugh.'

'I'm not sure I saw a copy.'

'. . . ? But you told me . . . in the window.'

'No, the book I saw in the window just had a woman's name for a title. *Emanuella, Maria*, something like that; with a picture of a girl in a headscarf.' I asked him the Romanian for wedding-cake; he told me. 'Well, I don't remember that one. But there must have been six or seven other titles by Petrescu and I didn't look at them very carefully. Perhaps it was there.'

Then we both paused, and looked at one another, and held the pause. I could imagine some of what he was thinking.

'Well,' he finally said. 'There you have it. Another piece of evidence for your Romanian theory. Another single bloom. One great ironist – Petrescu.'

'Of course,' I replied quickly, and gave him my most agreeing smile.

The Outsider
Nancy Oliver

It came to him under the door first thing on Monday morning.
It was pushed inch by inch over the stringy, puce carpet which
was provided for students' residential quarters.

He did not immediately pick it up, but went on with his
efforts at the looking glass to improve the large amorphous
face which no-one would look at twice. He wet a finger under
the cold tap and stroked his eyebrows; boldness and character
were what his appearance lacked. At ten he had an interview
with his personal tutor.

'They're early,' he thought glancing at the leaflet which lay
on the floor and listening to rapid steps down the long corridor. Last night he had opened his door to find two sad males
anxious to convert him to the word of God. Earlier in the
week there had been enthusiastic females who begged him to
fill in the answers to their questionnaire. They appeared to be
sociologists or psychologists, he was not sure which, but a
question which had caught his eye was, 'Do you always wash
your hands after using the lavatory?'

He picked up the leaflet. It had been photocopied probably
on the union office machine, which was open to the use of a
hundred or so sections and to a few pirates as well. 'Why
bother to vote?' appeared in capitals on the front page.

'Do you really want,' the leaflet jeered, 'the union executive
to be obsessed with the launderette, the crèche, and out-dated
slot machines? Is there nothing more vital to work for? Are
there no better causes? At a time when society is realizing how
corrupt and inept it is. . .' Several hundred words followed
ending with a flourish, 'Clear the decks now. Vote for
Superanarchy, the only way.'

He held the leaflet over the waste-paper bin then changed his mind and placed it on top of his miscellaneous heap. Then he forgot it.

The communal kitchen at the end of the passage was empty when he entered, clutching his mug in one hand and the top of his trousers with the other. 'I'm sorry but you'll have to wear these out first,' his mother had said when he had asked for a pair of well-fitting jeans. No doubt when he had worn out this pair, which were slack at the waist, in spite of his bulk, and flopped over his shoes, his father would be ready to cast off another.

'Good morning, Kevin,' came a clear, ringing voice and Jacqueline swept in. Behind her floated the skirt of a silk housecoat, fitted at the waist and flounced below. He muttered something and put the key in his locker and took out muesli and a bag of sugar. Jacqueline was a full-blown young woman, half French and half Italian, with a captivating Parisian accent, and he shrank into himself as she sailed over to the sink beside him. Her plump fingers on the tap ended in blood-red nails. She gave him her most generous smile.

Soon they were all, of both sexes, round him, weaving in and out of each other to the stoves, the fridge, the sinks and the lockers, some dressed but with bare feet, some in their pyjamas, and one who had jogged in the early morning in his shorts only. Kevin hardly dared sit down in such company, so he stood against the shelves fascinated.

'Yoicks, yoicks.' Strange noises came from the door followed by Adam, half clad.

'God, I'm late,' said Adam. At nineteen he could have modelled for Michelangelo's David. Kevin gaped. This was life, something he wanted to see and know more about. It was completely different from his home, that small house in Clapham which was dark, unpainted, silent and had a strange smell which might be due to woodworm.

They were in too much of a hurry to talk, and they were out of the kitchen almost as soon as they were in. He stood munching, taking in every detail. Whatever happened, he wanted to stay his full three years if only for this, to observe if not to take part.

Only when the last of them had gone did he wash his enamel dog-dish, turn it upside down on the draining board and go.

Back in his room Kevin glanced at the leaflet on his desk but still did not take it up. There was half an hour to spare before his interview. He ought to be reading for this afternoon, but instead he went to the window and stared down at the grass and the plane trees.

Something might indeed happen to him. He recalled with a shiver his end of term reports in December. 'Needs to do far more reading of the essential texts.' It all hinged on what you meant by essential, he thought. His idea of essential was so much briefer than theirs. He had been asked to go and see Dr Wells this morning and the interview was over and above the normal term's ration. It could only be ominous. He must make a fight for it or he would be taken from this Eden, this demi-Paradise.

He saw a figure struggling along the main path through the campus. Wasn't it Vic trying with a friend to convey his dinghy to a car trailer a few yards beyond? They would drive to the coast. There was a popular place for sailing thirty miles away. His vision of the good life extended into the horizon.

'Come in,' said Dr Wells. 'Do sit down. Why not take the armchair?' His room was so small there was little space for more than the two seats they sat on. Dr Wells started in the gentlest of tones.

'I expect you can guess what this is about. After we met at the end of last term it was obvious that something more would be expected of you. So far this term it does not appear to have been forthcoming.'

Kevin pressed his hands on the hard edge of the chair.

'The main complaint seems to be that you have not done your holiday reading. Have you?'

'Not much. My father was ill.'

'I see.' Dr Wells' tone became even more gentle, although

that had not seemed possible. 'And you had the job of nursing him, did you?'

Kevin said nothing. He remembered the one day when he had carried up a bowl of soup.

'I – er – '

'Yes.'

'I had – a few extra jobs.'

'What about term-time? How many hours, on average, do you work?'

Kevin thought hard. If he included the time taken walking to and from tutorials, reading notice boards, visits to and around the library, trips to bookshops in the nearest town looking at books he did not buy and never expected to read, he could, he thought, push it up to only two and a half hours daily. He said nothing.

'You see,' said Dr Wells, 'I would have thought – I may be wrong, of course – that in your position you could not afford to do less than six hours a day for six days in the week. Does philosophy not interest you?'

'Yes.'

'Do you not understand what you do manage to read?'

Kevin was stung. The thought that he might be incapable was not to be borne.

'Oh yes, I understand it.' He pressed the chair edge harder.

'What is it that does interest you?'

'I like the general ideas. They are very – ' he could not think of a synonym and ended blankly, 'interesting. It's the details which are boring, I mean – '

'Yes?'

Privately he thought that if an argument was obviously mistaken and had clearly been shown to be mistaken by other writers, there was little point in pursuing it. But he did not succeed in getting this across.

'I am not sure where you would draw the line between what you call detail and the main arguments. But if you have not done much reading then this becomes apparent in what you write, which can be very thin.'

Kevin walked back across the grass. The rest of what Dr Wells had said was lost to him. He remembered his own rising tension as the tutor sounded sorry for him. That he could not stand.

On the notice board was the usual flutter of paper. There were frantic notes from people living on campus who would be only too glad of a room in the town. There were people in rooms in town who couldn't wait for a more convenient room on campus. There were offers of cars, caravans, hi-fi and videos.

Among notices from the Health Bureau there were veiled references to various addictive drugs. The Bureau was proud of having largely overcome the great scare. Kevin knew little about drugs. They were, he knew, expensive and his small allowance was barely enough to cover even food. Perhaps if one took drugs one did not want to eat. LSD for example: he had read somewhere that it lessens the appetite. At moments like this he thought of experimenting with it. Would it be worth it? Probably not. He liked eating.

The Superanarchists' tract lying on his desk took his mind off drugs and he fingered it curiously. In what way were Superanarchists different from other anarchists? He tried to remember what he had read about anarchism in one of those tutorials in which he had been more awake than asleep. There was Proudhon, of course, and there were others. Bakunin believed in violence. Kropotkin thought class privilege and unfair distribution of wealth produced crime. There was Herbert Spencer, but he had not followed that trail. But more recently what had happened to anarchism? He must look it up.

If he wanted to stay here he really would have to work harder, he told himself reverting to the morning's interview. At the same time a large part of him was unconvinced. He would get by somehow. He was an ace at examinations and had never failed one yet. They stimulated him.

In the afternoon he and two other students sat in Professor Conning's room. As usual Robert was the only one who produced a paper. 'You write one every week,' Kevin had

once said to him in astonishment. After all they were required
to produce only four a term.

Robert now drew out his work with thin, delicate fingers.
He began to read. The mind, he explained, was in Hume's
view only a succession of sensations. We experience one thing
followed by another. Kevin noted with boredom the thickness
of the wad of paper. Professor Conning sat still and alert
making an occasional correction.

Eventually he said, 'Can you summarize the rest? We have
taken up half the tutorial already.'

'I'll try,' said Robert. His finger flew up in agonies of
self-expression. He went on trying for several minutes.

'Perhaps you had better continue reading,' said the professor in a flat tone.

Kevin looked at his watch. Only a quarter of an hour to go.
Was this really what was wanted, page after page of paraphrase, steady, accurate, but pedestrian paraphrase? No criticism, no assessment, no personal contribution whatever? He
tried to guess from the professor's face whether this was what
he approved of, but there was no clue to what he really
thought.

Polling for the new president of the union ended at ten that
evening, and Kevin went down to see what was going on
rather than take an active part. People were standing about
talking and a pre-Raphaelite maiden at a desk was handing out
voting papers. Among the by-standers was one whose face
was familiar. Kevin stared. This was the candidate of the
Superanarchists, the man whose face appeared on the leaflet,
Doug Braithwaite. Kevin examined him, walking round to
see him from the rear, noting his beard, his broad shoulders,
his powerful stance. He turned away and pretended to study
the telephone directories for a minute. With a suddenness
which surprised him he walked over and took a voting paper.
He made his mark while sitting on the windowsill, then put
the paper in the ballot box.

Elated he said to the Superanarchist candidate as he passed,
'You have my vote.' His arm was grasped and Doug said, 'We

must stand together. Tomorrow, eight o'clock in the science block basement.'

On any other occasion the melodramatic gesture and tone would have struck him as absurd. But now he was excited, he was in.

Before retiring to his room he made himself a mug of cocoa in the kitchen and stood watching the usual group round the table. Two had just finished playing chess. He no longer felt an outsider, he had other company to keep.

He spent some time in the library next day with the intention of finding out more about Hume. But he was soon groping among anarchists past and present.

At ten to eight he set off to the assignation. In the basement of the science block many of the doors were locked, stored with equipment, but one was empty and this was the most likely place for the meeting. Four or five people were there, a stack of lily-cups lay on the table and a pimply young man was measuring small quantities of coffee into them from a thermos flask. Kevin was disconcerted, but he put out of his mind the picture of an anarchist as a man with a bomb as well as a beard and concentrated on what was before him.

Doug Braithwaite stood slightly apart as suited his new status. He was now President of the Union.

'I was lucky,' he said. 'Few people turned up. They would not normally expect to vote until June.'

After the first congratulations, the group seemed over-whelmed by the responsibilities brought about by success. Silence fell.

'We had better wait,' said Doug.

A newcomer stirred his coffee with a finger and was offered a pencil by the pimply young man.

Kevin stared at the bottom of his cup and tried not to stare at the new president, whose face was like granite.

'Are you – er, evolutionary or revolutionary anarchists?' he asked.

As soon as he had said the words, he sensed they were a mistake. If he had not been one of the new faithful, the others might have hissed or snapped in reply. Doug said eventually, 'First things first. We must show we are a force.'

After another ten minutes they got down to business, some of them sitting on the table as there was a shortage of chairs, others standing. The new president had inherited a number of disputes with the university from his predecessor, who had resigned in a sulk. These already had some backing among union members and offered scope to the anarchists for exploitation.

'Our best bet,' said Doug, 'is the so-called Students' Encouragement Council which, as you know, is the laughable name for what is a disciplinary body. For some time the union has been pressing to be represented on it. Now is our chance to show that we mean what we say.'

'You,' he said to Kevin at the end of the meeting, 'will take the night shift. There will be no beds or mattresses, of course, so bring pillows and blankets and something to eat.'

They occupied one of the administrative buildings, and enjoyed watching the staff arrive the first morning and stand about helpless in the drive. But as the occupation continued, the staff stayed at home. Kevin would turn up in the kitchen on his own floor from time to time, grimy and excited. 'What is the latest state of play?' he was asked, and he would tell them before going to his own room to make up for lost sleep. At first he had his volume of Hume with him when he went through the side door for duty, but soon he took to thrillers and science fiction. The side door was kept locked, and was unlocked only after exchanges through the letter box.

'They've threatened us,' said Doug one morning. 'They say if we're not out by ten o'clock on Wednesday morning, the police will be here.' He stood with a paper in his hand, stern, outraged. 'Since they have resorted to threats, we will make it worse for them.'

Escalation was the main feature of his entire campaign. Early on Wednesday they would flit. They would occupy Irwell House in which were stacked records of students past and present. This would have two advantages. They could hinder a larger part of the administrative work than formerly, and at the same time examine the records for themselves. The whole question of records had aroused waves of hysteria among some elements of the student population, to whom they stood for incriminating evidence.

The early morning air on Wednesday was heady as Kevin and two others slipped out, carrying pillows, blankets and holdalls, and walked through the silver birches and over the primulas to Irwell House.

'How did you get hold of the keys?'

'We have ways,' said Doug.

Irwell House was at first sight a more convenient building for occupation. There were long settees and armchairs in the large entrance hall and the occupiers made themselves comfortable. The records, in the basement, were locked up.

'I'll settle that,' said Doug, but it took him a day or so.

Kevin tried to think of one or two people whose records he would be interested to see.

'Damaging material,' said Doug.

'But no-one likes adverse reports,' said Kevin, 'And they may even be deserved.'

'Do you realize that they can be brought up against you for the rest of your life?'

Kevin thought that if people brought up his reports against him when he was fifty or sixty, he would be past caring, but he managed not to say so.

But when the records were unlocked he went down to the basement with some curiosity. He looked up Jacqueline's terminal reports. One suggested that her essays on English literature were 'flowery and needed a stronger analytical content.' He giggled and thought how apt. Adam, surprisingly, was criticized for being too brief and formal in his written work. 'He should let himself go and develop his points more spontaneously'. Rather rash, perhaps? He then looked at the reports of a few other people about whom he felt less curiosity. Dust made him sneeze. After a couple of hours in the basement he was bored and returned to the entrance hall. He picked up his thriller. 'A better read,' he said to a fellow occupier.

The days and nights went by uneventfully. Something was needed to step up the campaign.

'Look there's the vice chancellor,' someone said one morning. They did not want to appear inquisitive so they stood at the sides of the windows and peered out. He was walking down the centre of the campus with a man who was pointing at Irwell House. The vice chancellor did not even look in their direction.

'He doesn't seem worried,' Kevin said in a flat tone.

'He's worried all right,' said Doug, 'but obviously he's not going to show it.' Kevin wondered whether his remark also referred to himself.

Once when he went in for the night shift, he found Doug and two others in a heated argument.

'It would be far better to go for examinations,' said one. 'The scope is greater there.'

Doug stood silent. There was a pink spot on each cheek which Kevin took to indicate anger. Then he began, 'I don't know – ' but remembered that a leader was supposed to know and stopped.

'We need action,' said one of the two.

'It's not developing,' said the other. 'It's stalemate. We're not getting anywhere.'

Doug, annoyed that someone else was taking the initiative, said at last, 'We must define exactly what we are aiming at.'

'We want a student representative on the examinations board,' said the second.

'We should set our own examinations,' said the third.

Kevin wanted to giggle again but held his facial muscles in a severe and resolute expression. Doug, now that his hand had been forced, went to the extreme, 'There should be no examinations at all,' he said. Then they moved away discussing tactics and/or strategy. It occurred to Kevin that the two talking with Doug had rarely turned up for duty in the occupation. Up to then he had been proud of his own long spells and glad to come. Now the first feeling of doubt came to him.

★

One summer morning Mrs Toddy walked slowly up and down the large ground floor room placing a printed sheet carefully on each desk. For the fifth time she checked that it was the right paper: English Literature, The Romantics. To make a mistake, she feared, meant disaster, and the example of the linesperson at Wimbledon was ever before her. During an important match calls had ceased to come. In the heat of the sun, at the age of sixty, and despite the discomfort of an upright chair, the lineswoman had fallen asleep.

'She appealed,' Mrs Toddy told herself once again, 'But it was no use. She lost the job for ever.'

A young man appeared at the door at the back of the room. She moved towards him. 'There's an examination starting,' she said in her holiest of holies tone.

'That was what I was going to ask you about,' he sounded deferential. 'I was wondering when it is due to end. Some of us have arranged to meet here this afternoon.'

'It finishes at twelve.'

'Thank you so much,' he said and she turned away and walked to the head of the room thinking, 'What a nice young man.' Such a pity they all looked alike.

It was not until some minutes later that she noticed something was wrong. Most of the printed examination papers on the desks at the back of the room had disappeared.

Outside the examination room the candidates were kept waiting. Surprise, mutterings and speculation grew. Someone had heard something, another had heard something else and the findings were put together or contrasted. Twenty minutes after scheduled time, when the papers had been photocopied, they went in.

Later, candidates were teased by gobbets of Keats, Shelley and Coleridge. Where did this come from – 'High Heaven rejects the lore/Of nicely-calculated less or more.' None of them, surely?

There was a plop on the window, a splash of campus mud, followed by a shower of earth and stones. The candidates looked up, their Romantic musings destroyed. The invigilator beckoned to an assistant, 'Ring the security guard, quick.'

By the time the patrol arrived, disruptive action was in full swing: 'Exams – OUT. Exams – OUT.' alternated with rock music on cassettes and record players.

At a post-disruption conference at Irwell House, Doug said, 'That was good, but we can do better.'

Back in the kitchen, between shifts, Kevin was surrounded and questioned. Never had he been the object of so much attention.

The Superanarchists planned their next big day with great care. As Doug pointed out, this time the doors would be locked against them, so they examined the window catches. There was one window at the back, a lavatory window from which it would be difficult to exclude them as the catch was faulty. They would wait until the exam was in full swing and climb through the window one at a time, Doug leading. Once inside they would put on face masks and create general havoc. It was a high window and they would give each other a leg-up. They worked out an exact order of entry. Kevin was sixth.

At 10.30 on Tuesday morning they met casually, as if by chance, outside the window. Doug was about to climb up but then suddenly he stopped. 'What's that?'

They all listened. After a pause, one said, 'What's what?'

Doug did not reply. A few seconds later he appeared to toss the thought aside, then his expression changed and he looked at Kevin. 'Up you go,' he said. 'Why me?' Kevin thought but he started to climb the few feet to the window. 'Push,' said Doug to the others, and they pushed, but this was a hindrance and Kevin lost his balance. He was spreadeagled over the window sill on his stomach.

Strong hands grabbed his shoulders and pulled him for-wards, and almost immediately there were urgent tugs from outside the building down below. He kicked wildly, freed his legs and was dragged forward through the window, the metal sill tearing his shirt and skin, until he fell in a heap on the floor.

'Are you hurt?' he was asked. When he looked up he saw the pink and white faces of two young policemen.

Sitting in the police station, waiting to be seen first by one person then by another, he saw only a slow decline before him ending in – what? After a while a word occurred to him – 'fall guy'. That was what he had been and the term suited him with its literal as well as its figurative application. In the next few weeks he saw Doug only once, in the distance, the thickset figure with a beard hurrying round a corner. 'We're lying low,' said another of the rebels by way of explanation. 'Leadership!' Kevin said to himself with a sneer. 'Bloody Superanarchists.'

He continued to wait, mainly in his room. He waited for his parents who were summoned to discuss his future, 'my non-existent future' he told himself. When they arrived, his mother seemed to be saying, 'I suppose we might have expected something like this' but never actually said it. His father's annoyance seemed to be concentrated on the cost of fares from Clapham.

Waiting wore him down and he grew irritable. He began to wish people would say what they meant instead of showing how tolerant and civilized they were. He wished he could have an all-in row with someone and then just go. But no-one would row with him. He began to hate the place and the people and was glad, now, that he was leaving at the end of term. In the kitchen they looked at him oddly, uncertain whether to say anything or not.

On the last day he happened to meet his personal tutor near the arts block. When the man said, 'I'm sorry it ended like this,' and added in what was meant to be a humorous tone, 'Keep out of trouble,' Kevin bared his teeth in a non-smile.

'Get stuffed,' he said as he turned and ran, not caring whether it was heard or not.

Only when he was taking a short cut at the level crossing did he recognize that his vexation was turning against himself.

Hidden Agenda

James Thurlby

They knew, he supposed. They must know now. One way or another, they believed he would go. The founding autocracy would be done. They would be free to enter the period of democratic squabble to which they repeatedly, if mutedly, referred as 'more modern management practice'. He prayed the company would not founder under the burden of it.

Sir Arthur sat back in his office chair, his body somewhat rigid, as if he did not care to make too much movement, took a white tablet from a dark bottle, put the tablet under his tongue.

Yes, he had been an autocrat. He still was. You cannot build up a company from nothing to a five-million-pound turnover without determination, without drive, without a good helping of despotism to keep everyone pointed in the right direction. You cannot hang about waiting for the blessing of a board's consensus view. You have to push on, motivate everyone else, carry them with you on the wave of your own self-confidence. And that was what he had done. And that was why he was chairman. And if today he still got his way in board meetings it was because they recognized only too well his pre-eminent knowledge of the business and the continuing force of his personality.

Or were they just waiting? Had his era reached both its physical and logical conclusion? He might know the answer to that when he saw the cardiologist later in the day.

Strange that Martindale's suggestion about the sculpture should have come up at this precise moment. Clustered around the proposal were messages he preferred not to interpret.

He was a pragmatic man but he was not averse to honours and rewards. One had just been conferred upon him. He had felt strangely humbled by it. Just as he now felt flattered by Martindale's proposal that a 'head' of the founder should be sculpted and cast in bronze and placed on a plinth in the entrance hall of the new office block.

'We are well into the creation of our own proud history as a company,' Martindale had said in his orotund manner, 'and to have a sculpture of you, Chairman, in our new offices will remind those who are to carry on of the energy and drive . . .' And so on and so forth. Martindale always overdid it.

In spite of the hyperbole, Sir Arthur was intrigued. He was certainly not without vanity.

When he answered, he had the odd sensation of appearing demure. 'If you and your colleagues think this is a useful and encouraging thing to do, I am not averse.' He was going to go on and say something about teamwork and the fact that the sculpture would symbolize . . . etc etc; but he thought better of it.

'I am honoured, gentlemen,' he said, when they had signified agreement, and smiled his thinly humorous smile which warned them not to overdo the laughter, 'that you feel my head should be on the block.'

Of course, it was not his head that was at risk.

Sir Arthur lay upon the sloping bed, like an anatomical hedgehog of pipes and filters. An angel with Asian features flitted in and out of his vision. His first thought was, 'My God, I have to have an operation.' Then he realized he had had one. A doctoral face hovered over him like a flying saucer. It said, 'Everything has gone well.' Sir Arthur drifted off again.

Apart from those moments when he felt he must cough and realized, always too late, that it was not an enterprise to be undertaken lightly, the return from the mists went a good deal more smoothly than he had expected. He found himself back in his private room in a seemingly short space of time, focusing badly but talking excessively (he had always enjoyed making speeches; he thought he did them rather well).

Sleep came and went; he was not averse to its ministrations. All the more amazed, therefore, to find himself being helped firmly out of bed by an attractive young lady in a white coat; and, a few moments later, tottering along the corridor on her arm. Tomorrow, she said, we would do some exercises. Wouldn't we? Arms and chest. He winced. And climb a few stairs. He gazed at her in disbelief.

After this Olympian interlude he was lowered gently into a chair and left to contemplate the course of events that had brought him to this situation.

'A what operation?' he had demanded of the calm but purposeful cardiologist.

'Coronary artery by-pass,' said the doctor.

Horrified yet fascinated, Sir Arthur asked questions.

He told the cardiologist briskly, 'I can't take six months off to recover from fancy surgery, you know. I have a company to run. Won't the tablets keep me going until there is more . . .'

'You haven't got *time*,' said the doctor.

Later in the same conversation he recalled asking, 'How soon should I have the operation?'

The cardiologist smiled. He was so much younger than Sir Arthur (at first, the policemen; now the cardiologists), assured yet faintly jovial as if challenging Sir Arthur to face a reality beyond reality.

'Ideally, tomorrow,' he said, 'Certainly within a month.'

A month, in politics or business, is a very short time, as circumstances had so often reminded him. It is a remarkably lengthy period in which to anticipate an attack upon your person.

Sir Arthur, despite himself, began to detach from the

executive matters which only a few weeks before had totally motivated and conditioned his life. He did not wholly withdraw of course. That would scarcely have been politic. He would ensure that his presence was felt for as long as he could.

Yet he was conscious that a whole new current of thinking was invading his mind. Like the man about to be hanged, Sir Arthur found the thought of the experience he was about to undergo concentrated the mind. But in ways he had not expected. Unusual questions surfaced. They seemed to rise from considerable depths.

Had his life followed the direction he had intended it to follow?

What a preposterous speculation. Not much he could do about it anyhow. Deal with reality as it was now. And right now he *was* the business. And the business was *him*. God willing, it would stay that way. He found he was repeatedly consoling himself. He would come through this trial all right.

However, his memory persisted in wandering about in a far countryside that he had not visited for many years. How odd to recall. As a youth he had had quite strong religious convictions; had even wanted to take Holy Orders. (Or had he just wanted to preach sermons to – or at – people?) There was no doubt he had always had a talent for enthusing others. Not too good at listening. Perhaps that was why politics had tempted him too! But, in the end, it was the pragmatic and the commercial that had fascinated him, the getting things done, the fight to develop new products of value to society. Manufacturing things. Selling them. These were among the basic creative and social acts of men. Pointers to development. Arbiters of change. This was his métier.

But the absurd philosophical questions continued. Was he sure his whole system of ideas, efforts and mores had been right – the striving after success, the competitive progress, the achievement. And wider still. Was the world being run in the right way? Was the market economy the fairest system for society? Was democracy working in the West or was it in decline? Did not affluence breed a kind of spiritual decadence?

Should man not fashion society so as to offer freedom but to require duty for the disadvantaged?

Fatuous debates. But, wait a minute. *Were* they not the big debates, surely? The ones you sidestepped as your life ran forward, open-ended, and you pushed on with the job in hand. It was only when you found that a precisely computable term may have been set to your life (even the smiling cardiologist admitted there were *some* risks) that you found yourself, surprisedly, toying with these deeper questions.

Problems such as how to ease old Dawson off the board seemed to assume less importance; as did Harrow's occasionally incautious public remarks, his getting into politics, contrasting so much with all his good, managerial qualities. And Martindale. His pomposity? Small problems, really.

He seemed now, by contrast, suddenly pitched in among imponderables. Meaning and purpose. Compassion. Responsibility of one man to another.

How many tendentious meetings had he attended, generating enough heat to bake the country's bread, but very little light, over matters of infinitely less consequence than these things.

All right. He would settle for this: behind every board agenda lay a hidden agenda. You had of course to have a raft of broad, generally accepted assumptions about behaviour, as individuals and as a company, about duties and obligations, social and personal.

But board discussions had to be practical. Could you fulfil the order from Saudi Arabia? How could you surmount the difficulties of trading through a government department of cast-iron bureaucracy in an Eastern European country? Could you conceivably invest in this new line of research when profits were so badly hit? What basically concerned you – yes, even today in the late twentieth century – was just one thing, *survival*.

Sir Arthur, to his surprise, began to keep a diary. In this he recorded his personal reactions to his situation and to the strange ways in which his mind was being concentrated. He wrote, of course, not for publication and creation of instant history (though he enjoyed the vogue for character assassination that currently passed for political diary work) but as a genuine, and therefore difficult, self-examination.

The prospect of the operation was daunting but he would not show weakness. He had the strange feeling that someone was watching him to see how he behaved; after a while he realized he was watching himself.

He wrote in an exercise book, discerning a faintly amusing aspect as his pen was guided by the ruled lines. It was as if he were a young man again, at the start of his life, with many paths of opportunity before him – scribbling in notebooks, seeking answers to all the unanswerables.

Did one learn nothing from life that the problems one had set oneself at its start should turn up again unsolved at the latter end of it? Surely it was 'unprofitable' to pursue such enquiries? He had been reading a little Buddhism, in a furtive and defensive fashion; he found it strangely reassuring. Also, he found he had a natural empathy with the use of the Buddha's word 'unprofitable' in regard to mental speculation. A practical man, too, the Buddha!

But the peculiar lust for introspection was not dispersed. Had he helped others? Yes, he certainly had. And he made a few firm notes in the diary of his encouragement of young managers and technical officers in whom he had detected the gleam of future promise. He had not listened to them too much. But he had pushed them on. Dammit, all his contribution to society had been through the company – and particularly to this community, for the local payroll now topped five hundred. Good products, balance of payments contributions, sound investment. What more was expected of him? Should he have been out in the streets of Third World cities taking succour to the sick and starving? Did not others do that? Oxfam? War on Want?

But what if he should die? Had he really shown love towards others? (He wriggled like an Anglican divine pinned down in a TV chair.) Answer, no. Except his wife. There were, in fact, many people whom he positively disliked. He even had maudlin doubts as to whether at this moment he could be said to love his staggeringly independent children. He had not shown the diary to his wife at first but then she had asked what he was writing. To his consternation she had wept a little when he gave it to her; but their sharing it strengthened bonds that he had tended to take for granted in recent years. They found a singularly refreshed delight in each other's company. The future pressed but they made new time for each other in each day. They dined out, just the two of them, in a restaurant which had nostalgic associations. They went to the theatre together (without business guests). They walked on Hampstead Heath. He was grateful to her, although he found it peculiarly hard to express his gratitude. Yet he felt she understood. That was good.

He was still going to the office but no longer for full working days. He arrived on one of his brief visits to find a gentle, bearded man in a green open-neck shirt and a jacket that had surely been through more than one jumble sale, waiting for him. The sculptor.

Martindale introduced them with his usual flourish as if this were the first day of the New Age. Sir Arthur smiled ruefully and said, 'Let's come back to the sculpting when I've got this other business over with.'

He reflected that he may have shown weakness, but at that moment the thought of his mute, immobile head forever staring across the foyer seemed too fatuous for contemplation. He found he suddenly had a distaste for immortality. And it seemed an inordinate vanity to assume that anyone should wish to contemplate his features when he was gone, whether his going were soon or late.

In an excess of sentiment (to which he did not altogether admit in the diary) he found himself sending off one or two cheques to charities which he considered deserving. Not conscience money, of course. Simply causes that time and pressure, he felt, had forced him to ignore. He even sent a cheque to a hospice for the dying (now and again, perversely, he felt in the category). His secretary was alarmed at first and then regarded him with a sort of reverence.

The month dribbled away to mere minutes. Clinical whiteness. Astringent smells. A nurse stuck a hypodermic needle into a rear quarter and the final moments of the month slowly and gently dissolved to a blur.

He recalled nothing more until he glimpsed the Asian nurse in intensive care. After her angelic, if distressing, ministrations were over, he experienced a further ten days of expert and compassionate nursing. During the first week he was acutely conscious of his own weakness and sentimentally grateful for all help. He felt as if he had done eight five-minute rounds with a large wrestler in a small ring ('Run over by a London bus is another comparison patients make,' said the surgeon cheerfully). But he was aware that some sort of miracle had been performed on him and he experienced a deep gratitude and found himself engaged once or twice in a sort of praying to, or, at least, man-to-man discussion with, God. He felt affectionate every time his wife came in to see him.

His colleagues trooped dutifully through day by day and he was genuinely pleased to see them. They were solicitous and even cautiously humorous. Peterson cracked a joke about the zip-fastener down his chest. Not too funny, Sir Arthur thought at first. Until, looking down at the stitches, he saw the humour was by no means inapt. (Peterson was an adventurer. Brash but quick. He could replace Dawson on the commercial side. It was the first business thought he had had. He felt, oddly enough, a bit scared by it.) His room flowered briefly into a conservatory of rare plants. In ten days, routinely, the hospital discharged him. He doddered to his car and submitted for several weeks in gratitude to his wife's care at home.

Gradually, his mood hardened. He was invaded by a healthily irritable resentment at the apparent slowness of his progress.

'You must move at the speed your body allows you to do,' his doctor told him. But his mind was way ahead of his body.

He found the acceptance of life, the moment-by-moment existence of pre-operation days slipping away from him. He was soon back with his old trick of living in the future. He thought occasionally of his former monk-like attitude. How had he managed it? There actually was a future to look forward to now. He was eager to get into it.

He felt he had got recovery by the throat. He could go for longish walks, he could potter in the garden. He wanted to get his hands on the business again. Were they really looking after things well? Had they been as keen as they should have been about the Middle Eastern contracts? Had they gone ahead with the research? How was the liquidity situation?

He sent for various people to come to the house to see him. A Prime Minister doing his assessments for Cabinet changes?

Martindale, who had been acting chairman, was surprisingly pungent and authoritative. What did Sir Arthur make of that?

Dawson came. Sir Arthur thought he put the situation to him kindly and charitably, but poor old Dawson went off like a dog turned out. Would he fight? Sir Arthur thought not. So he had a quiet word with Peterson. He began to feel Machiavellian.

He kept Harrow on a string, and was pleased to see how fretful the man was for power. Maybe he would look elsewhere. Sir Arthur hoped not. Harrow had a substantial contribution to make. Either he or Martindale was the next chairman.

But both Martindale and Harrow would have to possess their souls in patience. The present incumbent was feeling sharper every day.

He returned to the office, after a holiday in the Canaries, four months to the day after the operation. He felt good. He even felt aggressive. He already knew, slightly to his dismay, that they had apparently managed well enough without him. He had to re-establish his control.

His secretary fussed over him. There was surprisingly little for him to take action on. They had distributed his workload efficiently. Most of the board and planning papers he had already caught up with at home. A quota of personal and semi-personal mail remained. He would deal with that and then make his first appearance again as chairman at the board meeting. Speaking engagements? He felt the old temptation but turned them all down. An ambassadorial party? He grimaced. Two hours of leg-paralysing and jaw-shattering effort was too much to face. 'Ask Martindale to go,' he said with a grim little smile.

'And finally, this, Sir Arthur,' his secretary said, 'It arrived several weeks ago but I somehow felt you wouldn't perhaps want . . .' Her words fluttered away. She was disconcerted.

He reached out for the proffered letter.

'From the Hospice for the Dying . . .'

He was shaken. He had forgotten. The circumstances in which he could have written to such an organization seemed now so distant. The threat had been removed. The need for association, replenishment, reaching out, offering help (as a means of self-succour?) now seemed otiose.

'Did I really write to them?' he asked.

'Your own letter is attached,' she said, a little too quickly. He read both – twice.

And as he read, a strangely unreal yet compelling recollection came over him of the mysterious, encompassed days of his personal siege. Words he had scribbled down in an old exercise book. It had seemed so appropriate then. Yet the diary had stopped abruptly a week after the operation. The compulsion to record, to look inside, had gone. He had skimmed it once, rather unwillingly. He found the thoughts too quick, too near the bone, too naive, too confessional.

He had put it away in a drawer, hesitant about what to do with it. One day he discovered it was gone. He had an idea

Margaret had taken it, but he did not have the courage to ask her.

The letter his secretary had given him now was from the medical director of the hospice who thanked him warmly for his cheque and went on '. . . the interest of a man of your standing in the community is of great encouragement to us . . . if you wish to visit us at any time we can explain the valuable use to which your money has been put . . .'

He shook himself mentally and sharply and reached for his cheque book. The escape hatch. You pass from time to time through the valley, he reflected, but it is not necessarily your duty to linger there, though it falls to others. He had a board of restless talent to lead and he wanted to do just that. He felt the power in his hands and in his mind.

'How shall I reply?' asked his secretary deferentially.

He scribbled the cheque.

'Send this, and wish them well,' he said. 'Now I must hurry for the board. Let me have my papers please. Straight away.'

The old ring of authority. She provided his papers quickly and watched him go. Her face showed both sadness and excitement. She had heard a strong man speak with humility. And, after an absence, there had returned a warrior. She began to type.

His fellow directors greeted him with cordiality and respect.

'Thank you, gentlemen,' he said, acknowledging their expressions of regard, 'I am under instruction not to overdo things but I feel very fit and we do not seem to have a large agenda . . .'

It was his declaration of intent. He meant to take his first board meeting through to its conclusion.

He conducted the business briskly but precluded no possible expression of view. He was agreeably impressed with their progress. The Middle Eastern contracts were near signing. Someone had actually had a sensible and profitable conversation with the state buying organization of the Eastern European country concerned.

Harrow pushed for the new research to go ahead. 'A

company that is not expanding is dying,' he said. Sir Arthur thought he recognized the phrase as one of his own. He felt mildly flattered but discovered that his grip on his chair arm had tightened in a Freudian gesture.

The meeting was drawing to a close within the hour; he felt more exhausted than he wished to admit.

Before they closed, Martindale said, as Sir Arthur had rather thought he might, 'Chairman, under "Any Other Business" may I ask if you have yet found it possible to give thought to my proposal to have a sculpted head of yourself prepared and, if satisfactory, to be placed on permanent display in the foyer . . .'

'Good Lord,' said Sir Arthur, 'It had gone completely out of my mind.'

Conscious that he had told a lie (and feeling unrepentant) he took a long moment to look around the table, individually at each man.

'Well, gentlemen,' he said, 'do you all feel this is a precedent we should set? Heads on plinths – I rather thought that went out with the Romans. Is it your wish that such a sculpture should be placed in the foyer?'

There was a murmur of assent.

'If you wish it,' he said, feeling the slightest touch of humility mixed with a faint guilt at his own guile, 'then I have great pleasure in accepting and agreeing.'

There was a pause. 'That appears to complete the business for this morning. Perhaps you will take a glass of something with me.'

Martindale smiled. 'Perhaps you will take it with us, Chairman,' he said. And, at his signal, two waiters brought in glasses of champagne.

Looking down at his papers, still on the table, Sir Arthur saw the word 'Agenda' at the head of the top sheet. It revived for him the memory of something he had written in that diary so long ago: 'Hidden agenda' wasn't it? The deep things concerned with meaning and purpose. Were sculpted heads in that category?

They all raised their glasses and Harrow said, 'To Sir Arthur. Welcome back, Chairman.' Each was smiling, nodding in agreement. He, in response, raised his glass, noting and accepting, in turn, each man's gratifying and appropriate gesture of fealty.

No Angel Hotel

Anne Aylor

It was midnight. Elkie stared at her suitcase. On the side was a sticker of the Eiffel Tower. Another suitcase stood beside it covered with names of far-away places. It was made of black leather and had gold buckles and stitched straps.

Her cardboard case was dented. One of the catches didn't close properly and on the corners the linen buckram had frayed. The iron tower tilted towards the handle. She had never even been there.

The woman who owned the suitcase was a Belgian widow who had boarded at Bandol. After Mme Smekens introduced herself she unwrapped a box of chocolates. It was a going-away present from her grandson. The widow ate the whole box except one and offered the last square to Elkie. Mme Smekens smiled, holding the box in front of her. She shook her head; the widow insisted. She took the chocolate out of the box and put it in Elkie's palm.

Before she went to sleep Mme Smekens removed her rings. 'I always worry that when I travel thieves will cut my fingers off. I never give them the chance.' The widow had smiled and folded her naked hands in her lap.

Elkie flattened the soft chocolate between her fingers. On the floor were foil wrappers. The widow snored again. Elkie reached for the bottle of wine she had bought before she boarded the night train. 'It's not expensive.' The woman in the shop had seen her battered case; Elkie tried to stand in front of it. 'It's the local wine. It's very drinkable, mademoiselle.'

The lights in the corridor were shaking as Elkie walked to the dining car. The way the lamp had shaken when her father slammed the door. '*You have no business going off like this. No business. You don't even know the man,' her father said. He paced the narrow room. Only the lamp in one corner was lit. It threw long shadows across the cluttered room.*

'I'll run away then. I'm not a minor.'

'Not much more than, miss.' The finches in the corner began to sing. Her mother, in a limp housedress, held the wooden pole that supported the cage.

'What will we tell people when they ask us where you are? "Oh our Elkie ran off with her fancy man."' He looked at his wife. 'For the love of God, Marion, don't just sit there.'

'The darlings need more cuttlefish,' said her mother.

'Christbetojesus, cuttlefish!' They watched his shadow grow shorter as he marched across the room. 'Cuttlefish!' The family portrait slid to the right when he slammed the door.

The dining carriage was empty except for a man behind the bar. A glass case with hinged flaps covered plates of sandwiches and fruit. 'Six francs,' he said and drummed his fingers on the counter, anxious to go back to sleep.

Elkie walked to the back of the dining car to eat her sandwich. The salt and pepper tray was bolted to the table. She shook it. *'You have to excuse your father,' she said poking her finger through the bars of the cage, 'he's forgotten what it's like. You know, Elkie, when I was young I loved your father so much I would have died for him. Do you love like that?'*

Elkie opened her eyes to a dusty road running parallel to the track. The trees along the road were pruned like candelabra. The carriage was empty except for the attendant who filled the china-blue bowls with sugar.

Mme Smekens liked her eggs soft. The yolk wet her bacon and sausage. 'Beautiful morning, isn't it?' She pointed the handle of her fork towards the window.

Elkie had never seen a fried egg. She had always eaten hard-boiled eggs with yolks that flaked apart. Mme Smekens mopped up the yellow juice with her bread and leaned over to smell the roses in the centre of the table. 'Very pretty,' she said, 'but I can never see yellow flowers without thinking of my late husband. He was very superstitious. The ancient Egyptians used yellow as their colour of mourning. He wouldn't have yellow flowers in the house.'

There were mountains now, the colour of the sugarbowls, and fields of rye. Poles with sagging wire divided the land-scape like frames of a film.

The old suitcase lay open on the bed. Elkie folded a pink sweater and put it on top of the packed clothes.

'Now be sure to take a pair of scissors. You'll always need scissors.' *Her mother stood in the doorway. 'Look, sweetheart, fold it this way.' Her mother lifted out the tangled clothes. 'You can get more in if you fold them flat.' She shook the clothes out and made a space on the bed.*

'Your father's upset but he'll get over it.' She saw her mother's face in the mirror glued to the suitcase lining. 'All the same, Elkie, I wish you could have waited.' She continued, more slowly now, folding the clothes.*

'This is what I love about travelling, the breakfasts. I can't get my cook to make them like this. Indonesians are hopeless. They never get the eggs right. And the scenery. I love the scenery from a train.'

'You will write us from time to time, won't you? You know how your father worries about you. I'm putting a writing pad and some envelopes in the bottom so you don't forget. Just a letter every week or so to let us know how you're getting on.'

The widow put her knife and fork side by side in the middle of the plate. 'I'd better not eat any more. That's the trouble with getting old. Horrible thing, dyspepsia.' She stood up and shook the crumbs from her lap.

'I'll come with you,' Elkie said. She looked back at the table. The sun was melting the butter.

Mme Smekens folded her newspaper. Elkie pressed firmly on the writing pad.

Dear Ivan,

I know it is awfully soon to be writing but you left so suddenly yesterday that we didn't have much time to talk. I hope you have a successful business trip. I am on my way back now (as you can see the writing is shaky).

Of course it is too soon to have heard from you but I am hoping there will be a letter for me shortly. Please tell me, how are you? Are you massaging your toes? Excuse the red ink, the blue faded out.

Oh Ivan, I have so many memories now that I will always have! Do you know that I had never seen the sea before? Not ever. I didn't tell you the first time we went to the beach. The sea will always be for me like it was that first time, so cold and blue and frightening. I kept all the shells we picked up, the yellow ones that look like butterflies and the grey ones and the purple ones. They're all in my bag. I've never eaten so many exotic foods in my life and I'm glad you didn't tell me what the frogs' legs were till later.

I'm travelling with a Belgian lady who looks like the witch in 'Hansel and Gretel'. I hope I can find someone who speaks English when I get to Paris. The Belgian lady speaks good English. She can tell me where to catch my train if I can't find anyone else.

Before I left I bought a little book to teach myself French. I started studying it but the irregular verbs are so hard and the funny way the sentences are put together! The next time we go abroad I can understand the language and won't feel so strange. *Il fait un temps de chiens.* I said it to the Belgian lady this morning at breakfast and she was very impressed. She never gets off the train when we stop at stations because she thinks bandits will cut her fingers off. Isn't that funny? She has two rings, a sapphire and a ruby, and she takes them off at night and puts them in a drawstring bag inside her slip. She snores too. Did I snore, Ivan?

The weather's getting cooler the farther north we go. How's the weather where you are? Do you want to know something? You know when you got on that train yesterday morning, I had this funny feeling I'd never see you again. Wasn't that silly of me, Ivan?

I think I will stop now. You have probably had enough of my shaky writing anyway. Think of me, won't you, and write. Please write.

Elkie took an envelope and laid it across the writing pad. She saw the widow reading her paper, moving from side to side with the motion of the train. The fringe on the bottom of the window shade was dancing.

She finished the last of the wine watching herself cry in the mirror above Mme Smekens' head. It was so civilized; the red upholstery, the shiny brass plates, the varnished wood. She stared at the envelope. She didn't know his address. He had never given her one.

The station was open at one end, the glass roof supported by black-lace ironwork. Elkie looked up, not wanting Mme Smekens to see her face.

Mme Smekens waved for a porter. A small man with frizzy hair pulled a trolley towards them. The porter loaded the widow's cases. Her jewels were back in place, the large, cut stones shining in the morning light. The porter noticed the rings. The widow quickly pulled on her gloves.

'Where are we?' Elkie asked still staring at the roof.

'Why we're in Paris, of course.' The widow was agitated. The porter was staring at her hands.

'I mean, which station are we at?'

'The Gare St Lazare, can't you read?'

'I have to get to the Gare du Nord. Do you know – '

'And I must get to Antwerp. My plants must be half-dead. Goodbye.' The widow, escorted by the porter, went past. A wheel of the trolley caught her suitcase and it fell open. They didn't stop. Elkie watched them until they were at the gate at the end of the platform. They disappeared into the crowd.

She knelt to push the clothes back and saw herself in the mirror. Her mother had bought it on her honeymoon and glued it, for richer or poorer, to the inside lid. They had stayed at the Angel Hotel. They had a small room with a window overlooking the alleyway. There were the essentials: a bed, a wardrobe, a sink. No mirror or small bars of paper-wrapped soap. She had gone out the next morning while he was asleep and bought the mirror and epoxy glue and pressed it against the new sateen lining. She had wanted to see if she looked any different, how brides looked. *'When I came back with the looking-glass your da was lying in bed with a silly smile on his face and I knew how much I loved him and how happy I was.'* All the time she was talking Elkie watched her mother rub her hands up and down the front of her dress. She turned to look out the window. *'There are precautions, Elkie. I hope you take precautions.'*

Elkie picked up her bag and walked carefully down the middle of the platform. Near the doors was a flower vendor. Mme Smekens had said the ancient Egyptians wore yellow as their colour of mourning. *'Une rose,'* she said, her voice shaking, *'une rose jaune.'*

And Roses

Colin Beadon

Applewhite knocked and came in. He was in ceremonial kit. White tunic with silver buttons, black trousers with a red stripe, silver spiked hat of the island police force. He cradled something wrapped in tissue paper.

'My madam sent this for you, sir.' He would not look at the commissioner as he held out the gift. The commissioner came round the desk and took it gently from the black hands. He looked into the top of the narrow cone the tissue made. It was a bunch of small, fresh, red roses with water droplets still amongst the petals.

'Thank you so much, Applewhite.' He put them up to his nose. 'Will you thank Mavis and tell her I appreciate them greatly?'

'She would never have done so well without your assistance, sir.'

'Nonsense, Applewhite. She was doing well. It was just in the pruning.' The commissioner unwrapped the tissue, selected a rose, clipped it shorter with his letter opener and placed it in the buttonhole of his lapel. The colour of the rose matched the ribbons he had been given in Burma and his military OBE.

The commissioner sank back into his chair and finished his last report. It was a brief summary of thirteen years service in the island. The West Indian sun streamed in brightly and it was a sparkling clear morning now after a night of rain. Applewhite fidgeted around the office. The monocle fell from the commissioner's left eye. He was thinking of the garden party yesterday evening in the grounds of Government House. It had been his farewell and he would miss those parties and all his friends and the gardens overflowing with shrubs and flowers and the great vine-encrusted Samaan trees. But most of all, he would miss the roses.

From the square with its tall, shade-giving immortelles came the distorted blare of loudspeakers celebrating independence. They were holding elections, too, and he stood up, straightened his back, and looked down from the large colonial, shuttered windows at the happy gay-coloured, swirling mass. In one corner there was a more sober, tense group and he recognized the trade unionists up on a stage, under a red banner that read, 'The oppressed shall overthrow'. Well, it was all theirs now, he thought. They could do with it as they wanted. He turned.

'Did you verify the departure time of the ship?' he asked Applewhite.

'The deputy commissioner told me to tell you it leaves at one thirty, sir.'

'Thank you, Applewhite.'

'Will you be going back to the residence, sir, for lunch?'

'No. I will have lunch here in the mess.'

'Is there anything else I can do for you, sir?'

'I don't think so, Applewhite. All the kit is in the car, isn't it?'

'I couldn't find anything in the residence that you might have forgotten, sir.'

'Was Octavia still there?'

'Yes, sir. She is very distressed.'

'Thirteen years is a long time. I don't know what I would have done without her,' the police commissioner said. He was lighting a cigarette with lightly trembling, brown-blotched hands. The smoke crept up into his mass of profuse white hair.

Applewhite left the office, and soon after, the commissioner left too. He walked down the high-arched, wide, whitewashed corridors of the headquarters and turned in through a wood-partitioned doorway marked 'Deputy Commissioner'.

The deputy was at his desk. It was strewn with papers and overflowing ashtrays and ash particles spread by the great, slow whirling overhead fan. He was sweating and his shirt

collar and armpits were stained with it, and there was a wide
line of it down each side of the silver buttons at his chest. His
tunic lay over the back of a chair.

He put down what he was reading when the commissioner
came in and stood up, wiping his wide, black brow.

'Please sit down, Armstrong,' the commissioner said,
pulling himself a chair.

'I wish you weren't going, sir,' the deputy said. 'You
couldn't be leaving us at a worse time.'

'As you know, Armstrong, it's not my decision. There is
not very much I can do about it.'

'I know, sir. I just wish it was different. We've been through
a lot, sir . . . the strikes and the riots. But the background of
what is going on right now, according to the reports these last
weeks, seems the worst it's ever been.'

'I have always found you an extremely capable officer, Armstrong. You lack self confidence, and you will not get that until
you are in the position to make the decisions, which is now.'

'But I'll worry about whether I'm doing the right thing.'

'There will always be that,' the commissioner said. 'You
will have to learn to live with that.'

'Have you seen the reports today, sir?' The deputy was
wiping his face with his handkerchief again.

'I have.'

'What do you think?'

'What I always think. Take all precautions, don't get your
wind up, sit back and wait and see what happens. We've been
through times like this before. Remember that everybody is
excited, too. I don't know what possessed the senate to call
elections at the same time as independence, but then that is not
under our jurisdiction. We follow orders, and that is that. Not
that I did not do my best to talk them out of it, as you know.'

'The road the unions are taking is what worries me most,
sir,' the deputy said.

'They are a tough, militant, destructive bunch, I agree. But
then most unions are. They are no worse than unions in other
places, except for their lack of intelligence.'

'That's what worries me most, sir. The people under them are like sheep or goats. They believe all the junk they put out. I'd like to get one or two of the leaders in jail and cement in their doors.'

'Umm, it's a nice thought. Not very practical though. Those that came along to take their place might be worse.'

'At least we know who these are,' conceded the deputy.

Outside in the square two stories below, the excitement had changed to chanting. A cloud had gone over the sun and there was rain up in the hills behind the town, and a breeze ruffled the leaves of the palms against the woodwork of the shutters.

'The old order changeth yielding place to new,' the police commissioner said to nobody in particular.

'What did you say, sir?' the deputy looked up with startled raised eyebrows.

'It was nothing, Armstrong. I was mumbling to myself.'

The police commissioner was not thinking of the island now. He was thinking of the cottage in Devon and the garden he would make and where he would plant his vegetables. And some roses, he thought. And some roses. He would write his memoirs. That was a good idea. It would help to pass the winter. It would help to pass the time, all the times when he could not be in the garden. He tried to imagine himself in the garden now. But he had not found the cottage yet and it was difficult. Maybe I should have got married again, he thought. It is a little late for that though. Twelve years is a long time to live by yourself and my ways are set.

The heavy, black office desk telephone rang. The deputy reached for it.

'Deputy here,' he said. He listened to the voice on the end of the line. His face taughtened as he listened and fresh beads of sweat burst out on his brow.

'Thank you,' he said and replaced the phone. 'Mob set light to a bus downtown,' he said tensely.

'Is the riot squad out?' the commissioner asked.

'They are on their way, sir. I think I'd better go and take a look at the situation.' He looked at the commissioner searchingly.

'Armstrong, I would gladly go with you, but I have no authority now. There is a letter on my desk. It has all been handed to you.'

The deputy, who was now the commissioner, stood tall and solid, a great compact bulk of a man with a new weight on his shoulders. Strangely, the ex-commissioner noted, he had stopped sweating, as though he had decided to accept in a moment of inner strength the responsibilities that had been thrust upon him.

'I'm going to have to cancel the ceremonial departing parade, sir,' he said evenly in a strange, new voice.

'You know I hate those things anyhow, Phillip,' the ex-commissioner said. 'I would much rather leave quietly and with no fuss.'

'I don't know if I am going to be able to come down and see you off,' the new commissioner said. 'If I don't, you will know that I had wanted to, sir, and I am very grateful . . .' He could not finish the sentence. He was swallowing as though there was something in his throat.

'Goodbye, Phillip,' the ex-commissioner said, taking the great hand. He looked up into the face of the man who stood one foot taller than he did. 'I have been hard on you sometimes. Now you are in my position, you will begin to understand. I think you've understood anyhow. You are a brilliant police officer and I wish you all the luck.'

'It's been a great pleasure . . .' There was something in his throat again and the new commissioner turned aside and went out through the door.

He had had lunch by himself in the mess and he was on his way to the docks now and Applewhite was driving and they were going down through what they hoped would be a quieter street in the town. And then they came up into the thick, milling crowd with nowhere to turn and there was a steel band blocking the way of the black Jaguar with the police crest flying on the bonnet. The ex-commissioner got out of the car. He had changed to civilian wear but he still had his officer's baton with the silver knob on the top.

He walked chin out, hard-faced, briskly up to the leader of the band, his baton under his left arm, his right hand on the knob. The steel band leader watched him come, a small man with white hair in an outmoded civilian, grey suit and a public-school tie and trousers that flopped in the wind, and a small red rose in the lapel.

The steel band leader spread his arms and silenced the band. There was a murmur in the crowd and they pressed in around the ex-commissioner and there was menace in their faces like people who have awoken rudely from a deep sleep.

'I'm going to have to ask you to make way for my car,' the ex-commissioner said, looking up into the face of the band leader who was tall and barechested with a bright-coloured headtie and a tooth around a bead chain at his neck. The band leader placed his hands on his hips and looked down at this last vestige of the British empire. He looked into the eyes of a man who had seen riots and terrorism and war and death and all the vileness that man can do to man and he recognized and registered his value.

'All right, boys. All right. Let's move aside,' he shouted loudly; and he turned and started ordering a gap through the band. They fell back like the ocean rolls back on a beach. There was a strange silence in the crowd of black faces and the ex-commissioner ordered his car forward and then got in beside Applewhite and raised his hand in salute to the band leader as the car went silently through.

'I don't know how you do it, sir,' Applewhite said, running his finger into the collar of the tunic. There was sweat in a stream down his face.

'It's called "pressing your luck", Applewhite. Sometimes we have to do it,' the ex-commissioner said.

They went through into the docks and there was the liner, long and great and white, with the sun blinding on her sides and Octavia had found her way there and she was waiting at the bottom of the gangway, big and fat, her bushy, sandy hair almost turned to white, the lines in her face much deeper now, her old woman's eyes red-rimmed from weeping.

'Master, oh master, carry me with you. Carry me to England. What I go do without you?'

'Ochy, you know I would if I could.' He placed his hand on her great arms where she had locked them into the stanchion posts of the gangway as if she were trying to hold the huge liner from leaving. There was not very much he could say. There was nothing he could do to help her now. He could not say goodbye properly to Applewhite, and as he climbed the gangway he felt a tired, strange weakness in his legs.

Standing at the top of the companionway, he looked back at the island he was leaving. He looked up into the hills with the vultures flying like high, minute specks of soot, at the smoke haze over the town, at the clear, brilliant sea, at the Jaguar parked on the wharf, at Applewhite consoling Octavia, both of them with tears in their eyes, at the tall steeple of the cathedral where his wife, Anna, had been buried one year after they had come, at the high, hot noonday sun and at the flag flying from the top of the police headquarters where the years had gone.

There was the shrill call of a police whistle in the town and the chilling cry of a siren. But the battles he had fought were all over and these new ones were no longer for him. He was thinking once again of the garden in Devon with a view of the sea perhaps, and woods nearby, and fields and maybe roses.

Yes, roses. There would have to be some roses. There should be enough money for a few, just a few roses. But he was not sure what he would do through the long, dark, cold winters.

Going Places

A. R. Barton

'When I leave,' Sophie said, coming home from school, 'I'm going to have a boutique.'

Jansie, linking arms with her along the street, looked doubtful.

'Takes money, Soaf, something like that.'

'I'll find it,' Sophie said, staring far down the street.

'Take you a long time to save that much.'

'Well, I'll be a manager then – yes, of course – to begin with. Till I've got enough. But anyway, I know just how it's all going to look.'

'They wouldn't make you manager straight off, Soaf.'

'I'll be like Mary Quant,' Sophie said. 'I'll be a natural. They'll see it from the start. I'll have the most amazing shop this city's ever seen.'

Jansie, knowing they were both earmarked for the biscuit factory, became melancholy. She wished Sophie wouldn't say these things.

When they reached Sophie's street Jansie said, 'It's only a few months away now, Soaf, you really should be sensible. They don't pay well for shop work, you know that, your dad would never allow it.'

'Or an actress. Now there's real money in that. Yes, and I could maybe have the boutique on the side. Actresses don't work full time, do they? Anyway, that or a fashion designer, you know – something a bit sophisticated.'

And she turned in through the open street door leaving Jansie standing in the rain.

★

'If ever I come into money I'll buy a boutique.'

'Huh – if you ever come into money . . . if you ever come into money you'll buy us a blessed decent house to live in, thank you very much.'

Sophie's father was scooping shepherd's pie into his mouth as hard as he could go, his plump face still grimy and sweat-marked from the day.

'She thinks money grows on trees, don't she, Dad?' said little Derek, hanging on the back of his father's chair.

Their mother sighed.

Sophie watched her back stooped over the sink and wondered at the incongruity of the delicate bow which fastened her apron strings. The delicate-seeming bow and the crooked back. The evening had already blacked in the windows and the small room was steamy from the stove and cluttered with the heavy-breathing man in his vest at the table and the dirty washing piled up in the corner. Sophie felt a tightening in her throat. She went to look for her brother Geoff.

He was kneeling on the floor in the next room tinkering with a part of his motorcycle over some newspaper spread on the carpet. He was three years out of school, an apprentice mechanic, travelling to his work each day to the far side of the city. He was almost grown up now, and she suspected areas of his life about which she knew nothing, about which he never spoke. He said little at all, ever, voluntarily. Words had to be prized out of him like stones out of the ground. And she was jealous of his silence. When he wasn't speaking it was as though he was away somewhere, out there in the world in those places she had never been. Whether they were only the outlying districts of the city, or places beyond in the surrounding country – who knew? – they attained a special fascination simply because they were unknown to her and remained out of her reach.

Perhaps there were also people, exotic, interesting people of whom he never spoke – it was possible, though he was quiet and didn't make new friends easily. She longed to know them. She wished she could be admitted more deeply into her

brother's affections and that someday he might take her with
him. Though their father forbade it and Geoff had never
expressed an opinion, she knew he thought her too young.
And she was impatient. She was conscious of a vast world out
there waiting for her and she knew instinctively that she
would feel as at home there as in the city which had always
been her home. It expectantly awaited her arrival. She saw
herself riding there behind Geoff. He wore new, shining black
leathers and she a yellow dress with a kind of cape that flew out
behind. There was the sound of applause as the world rose to
greet them.

He sat frowning at the oily component he cradled in his
hands, as though it were a small dumb animal and he was
willing it to speak.

'I met Danny Casey,' Sophie said.

He looked round abruptly. 'Where?'

'In the arcade – funnily enough.'

'It's never true.'

'I did too.'

'You told Dad?'

She shook her head, chastened at his unawareness that he
was always the first to share her secrets.

'I don't believe it.'

'There I was looking at the clothes in Royce's window when
someone came and stood beside me, and I looked round and
who should it be but Danny Casey.'

'All right, what does he look like?'

'Oh come on, you know what he looks like.'

'Close to, I mean.'

'Well – he has green eyes. Gentle eyes. And he's not so tall as
you'd think . . .' She wondered if she should say about his
teeth, but decided against it.

Their father had washed when he came in and his face and
arms were shiny and pink and he smelled of soap. He switched
on the television, tossed one of little Derek's shoes from his
chair onto the sofa, and sat down with a grunt.

'Sophie met Danny Casey,' Geoff said.

Sophie wriggled where she was sitting at the table.

Her father turned his head on his thick neck to look at her. His expression was one of disdain.

'It's true,' Geoff said.

'I once knew a man who had known Tom Finney,' his father said reverently to the television. 'But that was a long time ago.'

'You told us,' Geoff said.

'Casey might be that good some day.'

'Better than that even. He's the best.'

'If he keeps his head on his shoulders. If they look after him properly. A lot of distractions for a youngster in the game these days.'

'He'll be all right. He's with the best team in the country.'

'He's very young yet.'

'He's older than I am.'

'Too young really for the first team.'

'You can't argue with that sort of ability.'

'He's going to buy a shop,' Sophie said from the table.

Her father grimaced. 'Where'd you hear that?'

'He told me so.'

He muttered something inaudible and dragged himself round in his chair. 'This another of your wild stories?'

'She met him in the arcade,' Geoff said, and told him how it had been.

'One of these days you're going to talk yourself into a load of trouble,' her father said aggressively.

'Geoff knows it's true, don't you Geoff?'

'He don't believe you – though he'd like to.'

The table lamp cast an amber glow across her brother's bedroom wall, and across the large poster of United's first team squad and the row of coloured photographs beneath, three of them of the young Irish prodigy, Casey.

'Promise you'll tell no-one?' Sophie said.

'Nothing to tell is there?'

'Promise, Geoff – Dad'd murder me.'

'Only if he thought it was true.'

'Please, Geoff.'

'Christ, Sophie, you're still at school. Casey must have strings of girls.'

'No he doesn't.'

'How could you know that?' he jeered.

'He told me, that's how.'

'As if anyone would tell a girl something like that.'

'Yes he did. He isn't like that. He's . . . quiet.'

'Not as quiet as all that – apparently.'

'It was nothing like that, Geoff – it was me spoke first. When I saw who it was, I said, "Excuse me, but aren't you Danny Casey?" And he looked sort of surprised. And he said, "Yes, that's right." And I knew it must be him because he had the accent, you know, like when they interviewed him on the television. So I asked him for an autograph for little Derek, but neither of us had any paper or a pen. So then we just talked a bit. About the clothes in Royce's window. He seemed lonely. After all, it's a long way from the west of Ireland. And then, just as he was going, he said, if I would care to meet him next week he would give me an autograph then. Of course, I said I would.'

'As if he'd ever show up.'

'You do believe me now, don't you?'

He dragged his jacket, which was shiny and shapeless, from the back of the chair and pushed his arms into it. She wished he paid more attention to his appearance. Wished he cared more about clothes. He was tall with a strong dark face. Handsome, she thought.

'It's the unlikeliest thing I ever heard,' he said.

On Saturday they made their weekly pilgrimage to watch United. Sophie and her father and little Derek went down near the goal – Geoff, as always, went with his mates higher up. United won two-nil and Casey drove in the second goal, a blend of innocence and Irish genius, going round the two big defenders on the edge of the penalty area, with her father screaming for him to pass, and beating the hesitant goalkeeper from a dozen yards. Sophie glowed with pride. Afterwards Geoff was ecstatic.

'I wish he was an Englishman,' someone said on the bus.

'Ireland'll win the World Cup,' little Derek told his mother when Sophie brought him home. Her father was gone to the pub to celebrate.

'What's this you've been telling?' Jansie said, next week.

'About what?'

'Your Geoff told our Frank you met Danny Casey.'

This wasn't an inquisition, just Jansie being nosey. But Sophie was startled.

'Oh, that.'

Jansie frowned, sensing she was covering. 'Yes – that.'

'Well – yes, I did.'

'You never did?' Jansie exclaimed.

Sophie glared at the ground. Damn that Geoff, this was a Geoff thing not a Jansie thing. It was meant to be something special just between them. Something secret. It wasn't a Jansie kind of thing at all. Tell gawky Jansie something like that and the whole neighbourhood would get to know it. Damn that Geoff, was nothing sacred?

'It's a secret – meant to be.'

'I'll keep a secret, Soaf, you know that.'

'I wasn't going to tell anyone. There'll be a right old row if my dad gets to hear about it.'

Jansie blinked. 'A row? I'd have thought he'd be chuffed as anything.'

She realized then that Jansie didn't know about the date bit – Geoff hadn't told about that. She breathed more easily. So Geoff hadn't let her down after all. He believed in her after all. After all some things might be sacred.

'It was just a little thing really. I asked him for an autograph, but we hadn't any paper or a pen so it was no good.' How much had Geoff said?

'Jesus, I wish I'd have been there.'

'Of course, my dad didn't want to believe it. You know what a misery he is. But the last thing I need is queues of people round our house asking him, "What's all this about Danny Casey?" He'd murder me. And you know how my mum gets when there's a row.'

Jansie said, hushed, 'You can trust me, Soaf, you know that.'

After dark she walked by the canal, along a sheltered path lighted only by the glare of the lamps from the wharf across the water, and the unceasing drone of the city was muffled and distant. It was a place she had often played when she was a child. There was a wooden bench beneath a solitary elm where lovers sometimes came. She sat down to wait. It was the perfect place, she had always thought so, for a meeting of this kind. For those who wished not to be observed. She knew he would approve.

For some while, waiting, she imagined his coming. She watched along the canal, seeing him come out of the shadows, imagining her own consequent excitement. Not until some time had elapsed did she begin balancing against this the idea of his not coming.

Here I sit, she said to herself, wishing Danny would come, wishing he would come and sensing the time passing. I feel the pangs of doubt stirring inside me. I watch for him but still there is no sign of him. I remember Geoff saying he would never come, and how none of them believed me when I told them. I wonder what will I do, what can I tell them now if he doesn't come? But we know how it was, Danny and me – that's the main thing. How can you help what people choose to believe? But all the same, it makes me despondent, this knowing I'll never be able to show them they're wrong to doubt me.

She waited, measuring in this way the changes taking place in her. Resignation was no sudden thing. Now I have become sad, she thought. And it is a hard burden to carry, this sadness. Sitting here waiting and knowing he will not come I can see the future and how I will have to live with this burden. They of course will doubt me, as they always doubted me, but I will have to hold up my head remembering how it was. Already I envisage the slow walk home, and Geoff's disappointed face when I tell him, 'He didn't come, that Danny.' And then he'll fly out and slam the door. 'But we know how it was,' I shall tell myself, 'Danny and me.' It is a hard thing, this sadness.

She climbed the crumbling steps to the street. Outside the pub she passed her father's bicycle propped against the wall, and was glad. He would not be there when she got home.

'Excuse me, but aren't you Danny Casey?'

Coming through the arcade she pictured him again outside Royce's.

He turns, reddening slightly. 'Yes, that's right.'

'I watch you every week, with my dad and my brothers. We think you're great.'

'Oh, well now – that's very nice.'

'I wonder – would you mind signing an autograph?'

His eyes are on the same level as your own. His nose is freckled and turns upwards slightly, and when he smiles he does so shyly, exposing teeth with gaps between. His eyes are green, and when he looks straight at you they seem to shimmer. They seem gentle, almost afraid. Like a gazelle's. And you look away. You let his eyes run over you a little. And then you come back to find them, slightly breathless.

And he says, 'I don't seem to have a pen at all.'

You realize you haven't either.

'My brothers will be very sorry,' you say.

And afterwards you wait there alone in the arcade for a long while, standing where he stood, remembering the soft melodious voice, the shimmer of green eyes. No taller than you. No bolder than you. The prodigy. The innocent genius. The great Danny Casey.

And she saw it all again, last Saturday – saw him ghost past the lumbering defenders, heard the fifty thousand catch their breath as he hovered momentarily over the ball, and then the explosion of sound as he struck it crisply into goal, the sudden thunderous eruption of exultant approbation.

Two Heads

Anne Spillard

At his interview he had been the only male candidate. The board had been relieved when he came into the room. 'A change from bloody women,' the chairman had muttered to the clerk as Brandon Shenley entered, closing the door too gently behind him.

His air of diffidence was timely, coming as it did after the confident aggression and undeniable dedication of the women. The education board by and large did not consist of dedicated men, and although they were aggressive, their confidence was assumed. The women knew this, and the men hated them for knowing. Furthermore, the women were well qualified, far better than the entire board, except the education officer, who was there to guide them. And the men resented this, they did resent it, even though they told themselves often that they were there on their intrinsic merit.

Brandon Shenley was junior to Nancy Simpson, who had also put in for the headship. They'd all sniggered at St Michael's when they heard he'd applied.

'Well, I'd sooner him than you, Nancy,' Effie Taylor, headmistress, had indiscreetly quipped to her. 'We'll be well shut of him, he can't even keep Junior One in order, and I can't do without you.'

But they'd all known he wouldn't get it. Creeping about, going out at lunchtime to get his mother's supper and the cat food. Never made a joke of course. People who can't keep order never have a sense of humour, Effie said, and by and large she was right.

But no-one on the board had a sense of humour either, and he got the job, and walked out of the room Head of Prestwich Road Juniors.

Nan Simpson had been there with the other ladies, and they had looked at each other aghast at the choice, as he smiled his shy smile, his blush spreading to his thinning brown hair. He'd hardly been able to look at Nan, and as he picked up his briefcase and walked awkwardly out of the room, he could sense the affront, and then, going down the stairs, he heard their laughter and sniggers. In the boardroom they heard too, but the reason for the levity never crossed their minds, 'Silly women giggling'. They gathered their papers up, satisfied with another job half-done.

Six months later, Nancy Simpson got her appointment: Head of Pound Street Juniors. News of Brandon reached her from time to time, and she sometimes saw him at meetings.

Her appointment was the result of logical progression; she had been deputy head of St Michael's for eight years, with a gap in between when she had been staying with her sister in America, a black space of years when they fought the mental illness of her sister's husband, and the only relief came with his suicide.

So back they had both come, where they belonged, and her sister got a typist's job at the education office, and she got her old teaching post back.

Four years ago. And now she was head, with her own office, shared two mornings a week with the secretary. But the triumph was a lonely one. She came back to a lonely house, lit the gasfire and fed the budgie same as any other day.

She tried to tell her sister that evening when she made her nightly visit to the hospital. But her sister stared straight ahead, not seeming even to recognize her.

'Only a few days,' the ward sister told her, 'though you never can tell the strength of the will to live. She could go on like this for weeks.'

Nancy looked at her lying there, tried to imagine the tumour like a soft coral, spreading into the brain, pressing, pressing. Her sister's head looked as it always had, with the fine pale hair, greasy and tangled now. Nancy took a comb from her handbag, and began to tease out the tangles gently.

Her sister whimpered, and Nan hesitated, perhaps she'd better not go on, the pain was probably unbearable. She put the comb away. Now one side of the hair hung down lankly, the other was frizzed and knotted.

But it didn't matter, because during the night she died. 'I didn't do it. Surely not, just combing her hair.' But she felt guilty about it, for ever.

Now the school became her life. She ruled, she was the head. They began to win things. They won the inter-schools netball, the Save the Countryside Award; one of her pupils won the Junior Art Prize awarded by a national newspaper. The school got good results with the 11 +, which Nan stressed she didn't believe in.

Nan was a remote head, with no friends on the staff; this would have been partisan. Snippets of gossip came to her about Brandon.

On his first day, Brandon had looked round his shabby office. He suddenly realized he didn't know what a head was supposed to do. He stood by the desk, looking at its dusty surface. He opened one of the drawers. It was empty except for the crumpled wrapper off a packet of coughsweets, and a small tide of grit in the two front corners. He removed the wrapper. From his briefcase he took a framed photo of his mother, taken ages ago, before he could remember, when she was twenty-seven. He put it carefully in the drawer, upside down.

Then he fished a glass jar from his coat pocket and put it on the desk top. He began to arrange pens, crayons, pencils, all from St Michael's, in the jar. He took great care, and gradually a thin layer of peace stole over him.

He jumped when there was a knock at the door. He was too self-conscious to call out, and, halfway across the room to open it, he was suddenly unwilling to do that either. He stood still, hands by his sides, hoping that if he didn't answer, the caller would go away.

But the caller was a seasoned monitor from Form Four, who opened the door and burst in with a pile of registers.

In the end, it was a relief; the registers were a regular routine task to be done twice a day. They had to be done, and made very little demand on him. He resented the days when his secretary, Mrs Peterson, came, as she tried to relieve him of this responsibility. The registers were an excuse not to do other things. Above all, they were an excuse not to make decisions.

Gradually the staff began to run the school. It was a form of anarchy that was fairly successful, and although Brandon himself took Form Four, and was therefore responsible for the 11+ entry, Mr Newby prepared Form Three so well that by the time they reached Form Four not too much damage could be done, and the success rate stayed remarkably stable.

He quite liked the days he had to attend meetings at the education office. They gave him status in the school, and at the meetings themselves, provided he stayed awake, nothing much was expected of him.

It was after an especially lengthy meeting that he had gone, with some of the others, for a drink. The divisional officer had shoved a whisky into his hand, possibly in the hope that it might remove the barrier of shyness and inhibition which pressed around him. The ploy had little outward success. Brandon remained silent, only answering briefly when directly spoken to.

The difference was inside him. He was no longer tight with worry and the vague feeling that something was expected of him. Impulsively he had gone to the bar and bought himself a second drink. It did not occur to him to buy a round. He would never have dared to stand the DO a drink.

Later, at home, he was able to bear his mother's querulous complaints and endless questions as to why he was late.

Next day, in the grocer's, he bought himself a half bottle of whisky, attracted by the flatness of the bottle and the ease with which he could conceal it in his coat pocket.

★

Nan was ruling the staff meeting. 'In the States . . .' she was saying. It was her chance to talk, and the others had little choice but to listen. This was the time she conversed with them, revealed little details of her life. She never mentioned the struggles with her sister's husband, the days and nights they'd been imprisoned in the house with him, him not daring to go out, and them not daring to leave him.

She did not tell them of the horror day when he gouged his arms with deep cigarette burns, or tore the put-u-up sofa on which she slept into small shreds.

Her days in Seattle, as she told them to her staff, were full of discovery and excitement. Such brief escapes as they had managed from the house were enlarged by capturing every tiny detail, and memorizing snippets from the local newspaper. She could describe Pike Street Market in vivid detail: the bright fruit and vegetables, the bustling people, the smell of flowers, the sweet scent of melon – they had never been to Pike Street, all her information came from a postcard.

Once they had driven along the dockside. From this hurried excursion, with Stan drugged out of his mind, snoring in the back seat, she told of the scarlet fire-fighting ships, the boats laden with timber for Japan, the luxurious ferries that took commuters to and from their homes on the islands of Puget Sound.

Names, she could use with authority and romance: Lake Washington, Mount Rainier, Snowqualmie Falls.

Mrs Peterson climbed the four flights of stone stairs to her office, to Brandon Shenley's office. She had nipped down to replenish the Nescafé for the staff's elevenses. As she passed the staff toilets, she shook her head. For a moment she thought she had heard snoring. She stopped. There was silence. She went on, back to the office.

Standing in the office, a monitor was waiting uncomfortably, clearly wondering whether to stay or whether to go back to her classroom. She looked in relief at Mrs Peterson.

'Mrs Bellamy says can she borrow the book on Animals of the World.' All the big, more expensive volumes were kept in a glass bookcase behind Brandon's desk.

Mrs Peterson opened the bookcase and took out the book. Some thing behind it caught her eye. 'There Glenys. Back you go.' She kept her voice brisk and practical. She went to the door with Glenys, and closed it behind her. Then she moved back and stood in front of the bookcase, looking at the space left by the removal of *Animals of the World*. She leant over and took away the books on either side of the space. Behind them was a half bottle of whisky. It was not full. She shuffled the books so that once again it was hidden. Then, half-expecting, she began to take the books from the shelf below, replacing each one after she had looked behind it. Presently she paused, letting out her breath in a sound that was half satisfaction, half dismay. She was looking at another whisky bottle.

Replacing the books, she picked up the Nescafé and went to the staffroom to make the coffee. She wondered whether she should send Mr Newby to the toilet to wake Brandon up for a cup.

At first there were sly references and rumours which you could discount.

'Not much use phoning Shenley after two o'clock. You won't get any sense out of him.'

Curiously, his staff, who had been so scornful of his in-decisiveness and ineptitude, now began to protect him.

He had had so little impact on the running of the school for so long, that little was required to cover up in that direction. Mrs Peterson took over most of his administrative duties. The registers now went to Mr Newby, the deputy head. Brandon had been surprisingly obstinate in resisting this. So, to placate him, they sent them to him 'to check' after the totals had been recorded.

He began to miss days, or to disappear in the afternoons.

★

Nan came to have the reputation of never missing a meeting for twelve, then thirteen, then fourteen years. At first Brandon's apologies were recorded in the minutes. Then he was usually recorded as absent from meetings.

There was a sort of initiation ceremony at Prestwich Road for new staff. At teatime, the staff would suddenly go quiet, 'He's gone,' and they would take the new teacher into his office and display, with a flourish of shocked triumph, the whisky bottles hidden round the room.

'I wish she'd bloody retire,' her staff would grumble about Nancy.

Brandon's staff were more lenient. 'They'll have to retire him,' they would sigh. They sensed that when Brandon went, things would not improve. Brandon united them in much the same way that strangers on a promenade might band together to save a drowning child. Brandon needed them, and they responded to this need. There was an air of purpose among his staff, who became noticeably resourceful and able to take initiative. There were no petty factions and dissatisfactions at Prestwich Road.

Perhaps it would have been different if Mr Newby had been more ambitious, if he had coveted a headship. But he did not. Years ago his ambition had reached its peak when he had played in the County Football Trials. He had not been selected for the team; but he looked back on the day of that match as the highlight of his life, and he did not expect the rest of his life, marriage, children, job, to follow anything but a pleasantly downward-sloping path. Coping with Brandon lent a little spice and adventure to his existence.

On the afternoons when Brandon went to sleep in front of his class, he had trained a Form Four monitor to come and fetch him. 'Please sir, Mr Shenley isn't well again.' Then if it was Monday, Wednesday or Friday, the part-time remedial teacher would stand in, after Form Four had been sent out for an early break, and Mr Shenley had been removed by Newby, and if necessary, Miss Atkinson.

Tuesday and Thursday were more tricky; Form Four would be split up between the other classes.

The children unconsciously supported the fable. 'We went into Class One today,' proudly said to a parent.

'Class One? What were you doing there?'

'We were helping Miss Atkinson. She said she couldn't do without us.'

'Where was Mr Shenley?'

'Oh, he was poorly. He fell over coming out of the office, and hit his head. He'll be better in the morning, Mr Newby said.'

It was also possible because of his mother. She kept him respectable; a clean shirt daily, his trousers pressed, ties sponged.

She fed him too, though gradually he was able to eat less and less. Coming home one day, he looked at the white plate with the orange breaded haddock, the fried tomato, halved between them, and the two oily mushrooms, and he vomited all over the lino. He had to go to his room, for he was shaking violently, and his mother was angry. He steadied himself with whisky from a bottle hidden behind his shoes on the floor of his wardrobe.

His mother nagged and raged at him, so he stayed out longer, or remained in his room. She gave up, assuming a hurt, offended attitude towards him.

Perhaps Nan's most endearing feature was her love of hats. She made them herself, decorating them for Open Day with big artificial flowers she got from the Co-op haberdashery department. In winter she trimmed them with little mink flowers, or bunches of suede acorns.

Her efforts were quite successful, and she would accept the compliments of her staff with pleasure and humour. 'You like it, do you? You don't think the green rose will be a teeny bit too seductive for the chairman of the governors?'

She liked a bit of veil, for a change; 'Imagine, there I was sitting upstairs on the bus, and I forgot all about the veil. Put this peppermint in my mouth, extra strong. I bit it before I realized. What a mess! Had to go all the way to the terminus, in case any of the parents saw me when I got off. I'm not giving up veils, but I might give up peppermints!'

Her hats gave her a Presence. They were partly responsible for her appointment to so many committees. You knew if she was there, at a meeting, and you remembered her.

Mrs Davison, chairman of Prestwich School Juniors Parents' Association, was holding a coffee evening in her house. The parents began to swap Brandon stories.

'He was sitting at his desk fast asleep. They were all walking about on tiptoe, not to wake him up!'

'. . . I just stood holding the phone. I couldn't understand a word he was saying.'

'. . . he just patted our Ronald on the back. And Ronald was saying, "Sir, you're drunk, sir, you're drunk." He never batted an eyelid.'

It was the end for Brandon. The divisional officer paid a surprise visit to the school. Mr Newby tried to intercept him, for half an hour they discussed the sports league in his classroom, but then the DO excused himself politely, and went to look for Brandon.

He found him in his office. He was searching for a missing bottle. All the books had been swept from the bookcase onto the floor. Files and cupboards had been emptied. Brandon, head in hands, was crying silently at his desk. He was, as the DO told it later, legless.

He was retired, five years early.

★

Nan began to make her own decorations for her hats. 'It's extravagant, paying all that for a flower that's a bit of tat stuck together with glue,' she said.

She bought stamens and berries on wire. In the evenings she sat at the kitchen table, watched by the budgie, fluting stiffened silk with a knitting needle. 'It's my only weakness, hats,' she would half-excuse her more exuberant efforts.

She began to experiment with big-brimmed, floppy hats. 'Do you think they're too young?' she would ask her staff, tipping her head this way and that. The cherries and poppies would nod precariously.

'Oh, well,' she didn't give them much time to answer. 'You're as young as you feel.'

Her hats became more and more extravagant. She would put fur and silk together with daisies and cherries. Bits began to drop off from time to time.

For eighteen months Brandon dressed as if for work and left home at the same time he always had done. He spent a lot of time in the public library, waiting for opening-time at the Crown, or the King's Arms, or the Swan. He was careful not to spend too much time in any one of them. In the summer, he sat in the park.

One afternoon he came home a bit late. He had promised to mow the lawn, and was trying to put it off. He hardly had any energy these days.

He was surprised to see that half the lawn had already been cut, very unevenly.

He walked round to the back of the house, went in through the back door. His mother had fallen across the table. On the floor was a broken pyrex bowl, the splinters bathed in beaten egg.

'It was too much for her, mowing the lawn,' the doctor said, not looking at him.

He was the only mourner at the funeral. As he stood at the grave, he wondered who would bury him. He couldn't imagine how it could be done without his mother.

★

'Miss Simpson! Miss Simpson!' Nan turned round at the school gate. Alison Smith, from Form Two, was holding out her hand. 'You've dropped your cherries, Miss Simpson.'

It was the second time Brandon had been found flat on the pavement. 'Don't keep bringing him in here,' the station sergeant told them. 'We don't want to muck out after him every few days. Just take him home and be shut of him.'

'It's terrible,' Brandon's shambling figure began to be familiar round the town. 'To think he used to be a head-master.'

Mr Newby, headmaster of Prestwich Juniors, went to see him. It was an awkward visit. The house was a tip. No washing up done; thick fluff on the stairs; a suspicious smell of urine.

'We've got to keep him occupied,' he told his mates at the football supporters' club. So between them, they got him a paper-seller's pitch, selling evening papers outside the Swan. Every evening he sold the racing results to his old pupils.

Nan's staff gave her a big retirement party; they even managed to persuade a few ex-pupils from the Grammar to attend, and a couple of mums, with babes in arms. 'Makes me feel like a grandma,' Nan joked ruefully. That's what she was old enough to be; that's what she should have been, playing with her grandchildren. Now she had to leave them all behind.

As she looked round at the faces all smiling politely, and answered the forced conversation, she thought carefully, 'This is really the end of my life. This is what I have achieved.'

She knew they were all waiting for her to go. She turned to her deputy. 'I'll stay and give a hand with the washing up.' Anything to prolong it, stretch out the thinning elastic.

But they were in charge now. 'What nonsense. Of course you won't. Washing up on your last day. What an idea!' They didn't want her. They wanted to be rid of her.

She went down the steps for the last time, turning to wave to them. 'Come and see us often!' But they didn't mean it. They had finished with her.

Brandon was on probation. It had been in the local papers. Drunk and disorderly, they had charged him. He had taken his clothes off in the street, left them on the edge of the pavement as if he was going swimming, then woven hazily down the middle of the road.

At court, as the evidence was given, he stood trying to remember why he'd done it. Vaguely he recalled getting ready for bed, making a massive effort not just to lie down fully clothed, as he often did.

The road under his feet, he could just remember it. He'd thought he was on his way to the toilet; he remembered being surprised at the grittiness of the lino. Then not being surprised at all, because he had become used to grittiness, fluff, grease, all the smells and sensations of uncaring.

Reporting to the probation officer every Tuesday forced him to be aware of the week's passage.

'Why don't you go to Nicholas House?' his probation officer urged him. 'They have quite a successful record.'

They'd dry him out. He sat looking at the floor, not saying anything. He couldn't imagine never having another drink. He knew that it would make no difference to his life, would not improve it, would in fact only remove the one thing he enjoyed.

Nan looked at the clock on the kitchen mantelpiece. 2.45. Time to get herself ready if she was going to arrive at 3.15. She mustn't be late, or she would miss the chance of a window table.

She put her hat on in front of the mirror, then gently shrugged her coat on so as not to disturb it.

Tea at the Co-op cafe. They would miss her if she didn't go. They always asked about her if she missed a day.

She smiled at herself in the mirror. People always wanted to sit at the window tables when the other tables filled up.

'No, of course I don't mind sharing with you,' she'd say, enjoying giving the favour. Then she'd say, 'Please do give your order first. I don't mind, I'm not in a hurry.' She was not in a hurry. There was all day. Sometimes, if she was lucky, she could spin out her tea till closing time. If she found someone to talk to, that is.

Often she would get to the store a bit early, and enjoy looking round the various counters, especially the haberdashery. As soon as you went in through the glass doors there was warmth and comfort.

It was warmer than home, where she economized with the gas fire.

Brandon left his newspaper stand on trust, and went into the market just before closing. They were used to him. He went to his usual stall. 'One egg, please.' The woman handed it to him.

'Six pence.'

He held the egg awkwardly in his hand. 'Have you got any over-ripe tomatoes to spare?' he asked. He managed to ask it with dignity, not grovelling.

'No we have not,' she said. ''Op it.'

He shuffled away, not looking at her.

She moved closer to her husband as he finished a sale. 'I'm not having him here no more,' she said. 'Bad for business.'

'He were a headmaster,' her husband said. 'Harry next door were at his school.'

'Well he's not a headmaster no more, and he's not having no more free tomatoes from me.'

Brandon was not hurt. It was a source of supply that had dried up. He looked round for another.

Nan couldn't see as well as she used to. At the hospital they told her it was cataract. It would be all right in the end, they said, but they had to wait till the cataracts were 'ripe' before they removed them. Then, with her new glasses, she would be as right as rain.

She sat at the kitchen table in the morning, when the sun shone through the window for a couple of hours before moving behind the house roofs opposite. It was the only time now that she could see well enough to work on her hats. The stitches got bigger and bigger.

As she walked down the street, people she could not see turned to laugh at her. Often the hats slipped to crazy angles; once she was dismayed to find, on getting home, that she had her green felt with the curved brim on back to front.

At the Co-op no-one ever sat at her table now. She began to talk across the tables to anyone who was ready to turn their face towards her.

The waitresses didn't want to serve her. 'It's not right, no-one will sit at any of the tables round her, have you noticed? It's not fair, if she's in your section you don't get any customers, no tips. And she gives you 5p same as she used to years ago.'

Most of them were almost rude to her, slamming her plate down so hard that the toasted teacake bounced on it, spilling tea in her saucer.

In the end, all but one of them refused to serve her.

'She smells,' they complained, 'sort of mousey. And you can't get away once she starts to talk to you.' Then they complained to the manageress, 'She's driving the customers away.'

The police had complained to Brandon's probation officer.

'There's no change. We still pick him up as much as ever. He's a liability. Always walks down the middle of the road at closing time.'

They were lenient. Several of them knew him because their parents had been in his class.

'That's what kids can turn you into,' the station sergeant would say, shaking his head. 'Take him home. We don't want him here.'

'He'll lose his job if we send him away,' the probation officer warned.

But, in the end, he had a spell in Nicholas House. 'We can only take you if you are willing to give it up,' the doctor told him when he was admitted. They knew it was hopeless, a last resort.

Brandon sat in the lounge, staring ahead, talking to no-one, or looking blankly at the television. The nurses had to feed him, spooning soft food into his mouth; he couldn't be bothered with anything he had to chew. They gave him multivitamins, at first by injection because he wouldn't swallow the tablets, just held them in his mouth till he forgot they were there and they dribbled out.

He smelt permanently of Heminevrin, which they gave him from a medicine cup, holding it to his mouth, supporting his lower jaw, making sure he drank it.

He was gentle and courteous, and, as he improved a bit, he did as he was told. The nurses were sorry to see him go.

'I'm afraid you can't come here any more.' The manageress had waited till closing time. Nan was gathering up her scarf, and the contents of her handbag, which had fallen out as she picked it up.

Her first thought was that they must be closing down.

'Oh, I shall miss you,' she said, unaware. 'Funny, closing down. There always seem to be plenty of people here.'

The manageress had prepared her speech. 'We're not closing down. You upset the customers. Keep talking to them and interfering in their conversations. And the waitresses are complaining. You use up a whole table every afternoon. They lose customers and we can't afford it.'

Nan drew herself up. 'I've never been so insulted. I shall be writing to the managing director,' she said. 'I must be mistaken. I thought the Co-op belonged to all of us. I have been a shareholder for many years. I shall be withdrawing my custom as of now.'

She walked out, bumping into a table, stubbing her toe on a chair. Tears which she tried to swallow made it even more difficult to see.

It was the task of the community health officer to clean up Brandon's house.

'We should use a mask for this lot,' the cleaners complained. But the pattern was familiar to them: carpets soaked with urine, mattress unspeakable, to be burned; bottles and crockery everywhere. It took three days to clear it up. They replaced the mattress, sluiced down the now-bare boards and the lino with Lysol.

Brandon was a problem; too young for an old people's home, not yet 'mentally ill'. They arranged for a home help to visit him regularly when he came home. And the psychiatric social worker added him to her overburdened list. Brandon was taken in tow by the State.

Perhaps it would have worked out if he had been given his job back. But the number of papers he sold had declined steadily, and during his absence the distributors had decided it was not worth maintaining his pitch as an outlet.

Nan sat in the window of the Priory teashop. It was nicer here, being on a level with the pavement; she could see things going on. And the waitress, the same one every day, seemed pleasant enough. The seats were more comfortable than the Co-op too, wheelbacks, each with its padded seat. A change was as good as a rest. She told herself she was relieved not to have to go to the Co-op every day. All those stairs to come down. They gave you an escalator to go up, but once you'd spent your money they didn't care what happened to you, and you had to come down under your own steam.

Something attracted her attention outside. People were standing about in that uneasy manner that means something bad is happening. She brushed her eyes, trying to clear the blurry vision that was like mist on a window-pane.

A darker blur, a man, was lying in the road. Cars had stopped. Then some of the crowd began to drag the man to the pavement. People milled about, consulting each other. Then drivers got back into their cars, and the traffic began to flow again. A few people stood by the man looking down at him, shaking their heads, discussing him. Then they too began to move away. The man lay still on the pavement. People passed by, looking.

Nan stood up. She walked to the door, leaving her things. It really was too bad. You couldn't ignore someone like that.

'I'll be back in a minute to pay,' she said, and went outside.

She walked across the pavement and bent down.

'Are you all right?' she asked, getting authority into her voice. The question seemed inadequate. There was no reply.

She bent over and shook his shoulder. The man turned onto his back and stared blankly at her.

'Mr Shenley!' She was shocked. She knew, of course about his plight, but this was the first time she had come face to face with it.

For a moment they stared at each other. Then Brandon recognized her. 'Miss Simpson.' A tiny crack opened in his mind. He should be embarrassed. 'Not feeling too good,' he mumbled.

'Sit up!' Nan said firmly. 'You could choke lying down like that. Come along, sit up.'

But his eyes stayed closed. She put her hand under his armpit, trying to pull him towards a lamp-post where she could prop him up. They were a bizarre sight, an old lady in headgear that resembled an Australian cowman's hat with its corks bobbing round the brim to ward off flies, pulling this dishevelled drunk inch by inch along the pavement.

A girl passing by put down her parcels and took the other shoulder. Together they managed to prop Brandon up. 'Now what are you going to do?' the girl asked Nan. 'The police will take him if he stays here.'

Vestiges of authority came back to Nan. 'It's all right,' she said. 'I'll handle it. Stay with him a minute.'

She went back into the teashop. The waitresses had been watching from the window. 'Can you please call a taxi?' Nan asked them firmly. They did. They assumed Brandon was some sort of relative of hers. It seemed quite possible.

Nan paid her bill, and went outside to wait with Brandon. At the door she called back to them, 'I may not be able to come in so often now. I may be busy.'

Standing by Brandon at the roadside while they waited for the taxi, she saw him open his eyes. He was looking at her. She bent down to him. 'It's all right, don't worry. I'm taking you home with me. Then you can have a nice cup of tea and a good long sleep.' She wasn't sure about the tea, whether it was a good idea. But he sensed her assurance. 'You're very kind,' he mumbled.

The taxi drew up at the kerb. As they bundled him inside, he tried to draw back for her. 'After you,' he muttered.

'That'll come later,' Nan said briskly.

The taxi set off, and she settled back, seeing the dim shape of Brandon's figure slumped in the other corner.

It seemed to her that she could see better, that she felt stronger, more capable altogether. 'There's a lot to be done,' she thought.

She was pleased that there was.

For the Sake of the School
John Rudge

Yes, Copeland's the man, thought the headmaster, crossing to the desk while the hissing of his private lavatory subsided behind the oak panelling. He pressed the button to change the light outside the door from red to green and sat back in his chair. Outside the mock-Tudor bay windows a light drizzle darkened the main drive and the walls of the physics lab.

He said 'Come' to the knock at the door and watched as Copeland entered.

'Morning, Head.' Wheezing, his cheeks the colour of port, Copeland approached in a stiff-backed strut. The effort to preserve a military bearing and his dignity despite the wobbling paunch and jutting rump was apparent.

Grotesque, thought the headmaster. Bulging fore and aft and still playing the major. That had been wartime, of course, but it was a decent regiment. He struggled to remember which, and noticed how savagely tight the leather belt was drawn under Copeland's overhanging belly. He had not conceded one notch on that belt to the passage of twenty years. The man must be in pain.

'My dear chap,' he smiled and waved at the chair in front of the desk. Even his clothes, the tweed jacket, olive shirt and woollen tie, suggested the retired officer. Yet there had been a time when Copeland had worn a suit regularly. Did he still resent not being made head of modern languages? The Greenjackets? Was that it? No.

Copeland sat down and fingered his moustache, which had the shape and colour of a worn toothbrush. His gaze shifted to the windows.

'Cricket will be off, I fancy,' he said.

'Yes, I dare say.' The headmaster watched the small, round

eyes. There was a trace of alarm in their vulnerable, watery blue. The florid cheeks slid down to the jowls, spilling softly over the shirt collar. Was he drinking during the day? He touched the papers in front of him by the tips of his little fingers. He remembered the boys' nickname for Copeland, 'Fanny'.

'I asked you to come along because the most disturbing reports have been reaching me.' He looked up and caught the slight jerk of Copeland's chin, as if in response to the cold touch of a pistol. 'Reports of perverse activities taking place between the boys in the showers.' He paused. 'Not unknown, of course, among adolescents, but distressing nonetheless.'

Copeland nodded sternly, 'Quite.'

'It would seem that a few individuals are exerting a malign influence.' He leaned forward. 'I fear for the moral welfare of the whole Upper Fifth and Sixth.' His eyes rested on the grey crinkles of Copeland's hair, kept neat with the fastidious vanity of the ageing bachelor.

'I had no idea – '

'No, of course not, no reason why you should. But I think some action on our part is called for.'

'Yes indeed.'

'It's a question really of striking a balance between . . .' The headmaster glanced at the windows before focusing again on Copeland. 'One wants to deal firmly with this business without getting it out of proportion, do you see?'

'I quite understand.'

'Yes, I thought you would,' said the headmaster quickly. 'That's why I'd like you to speak to the upper forms.'

Copeland's jaw sagged, making his chins swell. His eyes blinked rapidly.

'I'm not sure whether I would be . . . I don't know whether . . .'

'Moral authority, you see,' the headmaster pronounced the words with slow emphasis. 'That's the key to it.'

'Well, I must say it's very gratifying that you should ask me, Headmaster, but perhaps there are better . . . more – '

The headmaster shook his head and smiled. 'No doubt in my mind, my dear chap. Respect, you see, that's what it boils down to. Get them altogether and confront it head on. Put these devils to shame.'

'Did you have an idea as to what should be . . .' Copeland spread his hands, '. . . said?'

'Leave it to you, dear fellow. Own judgment.' He stood up. 'Tomorrow morning after prayers? Would that be all right?'

'Tomorrow? Er, yes, of course.'

'Good. First rate. I'll have them stay behind in Hall.' He walked with Copeland towards the door. 'I'm very grateful to you for taking this on, you know. Not an easy task, but . . . mustn't be allowed to fester, this sort of thing.' He raised one hand, fingers clenched, and jabbed forwards for emphasis. 'Get it out in the open.' Jab. 'Clear the air.' Jab. 'For the school's sake.'

As Copeland came out of the head's study, the bell for the end of the second period sprang into life with a jar like a burglar alarm. He heard the dull scrape of several hundred chairs being pushed back and braced himself subconsciously for the coming stampede. He kept seeing the head's face, his sickly, thin-lipped smile and pasty skin above the dog collar. The hollow cheeks gave his features the look of a skull, making the wide smile hideous and ingratiating. The stairs rumbled and Copeland hurried down the corridor towards the safety of the common room. In all the years he had known him, the head had never lost the benign leer of the vicar at the church door. It marked him out more clearly than the dog collar. He wondered why he had been chosen, and couldn't help feeling suspicious. Perhaps it was just that he was one of the oldest members of staff and Kershaw, the deputy head, was too ill to handle anything more than first-year Latin. Another post he need not apply for when Kershaw's heart finally gave out. Was it possible that he exuded moral authority? After twenty years at the school, perhaps it was. He would have to work out something to say to them. It was part of the job after all. He had dealt with a case in the regiment. As he tried to remember what he had said then, the roar ahead grew louder and the tide of navy blue blazers swept round the end of the corridor. They slowed down on seeing him, but in two sharp paces he was at the common room. Puffing and flustered, he reached thankfully for the door handle. Among their watchful whispers he heard, 'There's Fanny.' God how he hated that name.

After prayers the headmaster made his exit down the central aisle and the masters peeled off as he passed to follow him two by two in a wake of flapping black gowns. They looked straight ahead, ignoring the boys and holding their thicker versions of the hymn book tight against their ribs. The prefects stood in line abreast beneath the stage and glowered at the school. When the masters had left, the head prefect made a right turn and went briskly up the steps on to the stage.

'Upper Fifth and Sixth are to remain behind.' He looked at a slip of paper. 'And Watkins, J. is to see me at Break.' He came down the steps in a rapid clatter of heels and led a second procession of his cohorts down the aisle to the rear doors. The lower forms filed out, letting the canvas and metal chairs screech and crash. The older boys remained seated in the back rows. Their subdued conversation stopped as they became aware of the prefects returning and lining up against the wall behind them. Like alert but not yet uneasy prisoners, the boys assessed the signs and waited.

Copeland hitched at the shoulders of his gown and listened. If he left it much longer they would start talking again. The job was beyond him he thought, as he always did, as he had in the war, and marched firmly into the hall.

He heard the head prefect call, 'Stand up' as he entered, and the instant rattling of chairs. By the time he reached the first row they were all on their feet, interest and curiosity stirring briefly as they noted who was to address them. He stopped,

turned round, and told them to sit down. After this, he would
have a drink. The prefects remained standing, feet apart,
hands clasped behind them. Not chosen for their looks, he
thought. With the possible exception of the head prefect, who
was watching him, he realized, with a look of shrewd contempt. He was flustered and looked away while he waited for
them to settle down. The pompous little prig.

'I have been asked by the headmaster to speak to you . . .' –
someone dropped a hymn book and he waited for it to be
picked up – 'about the activities of certain boys in the showers
after games.' He sounded ludicrous to himself, but their faces
showed no amusement, only mild surprise. He tried to infuse
more anger into his voice. 'It is a shock and a disappointment
to encounter such disgraceful behaviour in the school. It will
not be tolerated.' Under his flushed glare they shifted with
embarrassment. There were looks in the direction of two boys
who sat together and stared stiffly ahead with reddening faces.
Copeland recognized Mitchell, the dark-haired one with
large, soft brown eyes. Above average French, he remembered. The boy's eyes were remarkable. Deliberately he
looked away. 'Any boy caught indulging in these disgusting
. . . these filthy practices will be severely punished.' As he said
it, making an effort to make the threat seem unimaginably
dire, he saw that they were looking at him with distaste and
something like pity. He paused, glanced at the prefects and
caught the same look there, and knew that this had been the
headmaster's intention. He was being put on show. His func-
tion was to present them with the spectacle of himself: an
ageing, fat, pathetic, posturing – he struggled with the word –
'queer'. One good look at him would be sufficient deterrent.
He felt weak. He could see the head's ghastly thin-lipped leer.
For the sake of the school he was being humiliated and
ridiculed after twenty years. He could see in their faces that it
was working. His hands trembled. He looked over their
heads, away from their eyes, and barked out, 'That is all.'
They watched with the usual slight amusement as he squared
his shoulders and strutted down the aisle.

Swallows

Morris Lurie

For a time in the mid-sixties I lived in Tangier. It was a good time to be there. It was an easy place to live. It was like nowhere I had ever been before. And it was cheap. Food was cheap, and so was where I stayed. My room and breakfast were about ten dollars a week. The fatima who came in every day made my room and washed my clothes, and whenever I wanted a hot shower she connected up the gas cylinder in the bathroom – an unwieldy business – and laid out a pile of fresh towels, thick white towels, smelling of sun. There was a slight extra charge for this, but nothing, really, hardly anything at all. Totted up each week it came to perhaps another two dollars. And travel was cheap: the Moroccan buses, the ferry to Gibraltar and Spain. By bus I went to Meknes, to Rabat and Fez. I went to Ceutta, that Spanish town on the Moroccan mainland, and bought Spanish brandy, smoked ham and sausage. And once a week I went to Gibraltar and Spain. The border between them was open then; all you needed was your passport. The formalities were a matter of minutes. You walked across. The ferry to Algeciras left at nine in the morning, was across the Strait in a little over two hours, the one back left at three or four in the afternoon. It was a heady feeling. You had been in three countries in the one day.

Where I lived in Tangier was not exactly a hotel. It was a dozen rooms off both sides of a long cold corridor, where all through the night the tap of high heels reverberated like metronomes on a grand piano. First there would be a buzz at the front door – that clamorous electric buzzer – and then that sound, that tapping. Señor Adolfo, the small, nervously smiling Spaniard who owned the place, called it a pensione, but of course it wasn't that. The rooms were rented out by the hour. And I was there to lend respectability: writer-in-residence in a house of assignation in Tangier, as I boastfully wrote to friends at home, hardly believing it myself. But it was true. The whores tapped with their heels, I tapped on my portable Olivetti; a household at work.

But my position in Señor Adolfo's pensione was not unique. There was another writer there, too, a tall frail Englishman named Orford St John. Orford had the bearing and manners – the correctness – of an Old Etonian, or anyway of some similar public school, but overlaid with the fussiness of age. He was in his sixties, wispy white haired, a homosexual. He was there when I arrived, had been there for about six months, living in the little room to the left just past the front door, and he welcomed my company. He seemed to have few friends. He showed me around the town, walking stiffly in a huge straw hat. He showed me the markets and bazaars, the cafés, the cheapest places to eat, the places to avoid, he opened up for me the labyrinth of the medina. He pointed out the mosques, the bathhouse, the famous places. He knew the history. He had discovered Tangier in the thirties, and now, retired (although I never learnt from what), he had come here to live. He smiled. 'Like an aged spinster eking out her days,' he said. He was not well. He suffered from palpitations of the heart, 'the flutters', as he called them. His hands trembled. On the slightest hill we would have to stop while he caught his breath. Then we would sit down somewhere and order mint tea, blinking and trembling Orford delighting me with the gossip of the town, retailing it with that wonderful maliciousness of someone who has not been invited to the party.

Occasionally we drank a glass or two of white wine together in a small out-of-the-way bar run by another Spaniard, Benito. I would knock on Orford's door around six, and then wait – he always took a long time – while he got himself together. Many times my knock would wake him from an afternoon sleep. He would awake dazed, his wispy hair flying in disarray. 'Ten minutes,' he would call. 'Can you give me ten minutes?' He usually took longer. I would stand in the corridor and wait, listening to him fussing. 'Oh, where are my shoes?' I would hear his crying. 'Oh God, now they've stolen my shoes.' But finally he would emerge, wearing his huge straw hat, even though the sun was going or had already gone down, and together we would walk to Benito's bar. We would sit there for about an hour, on stools, at the counter, drinking our wine, eating the *tapas* that came with it: small plates of olives or fried calamari or grilled anchovies or sardines. An old record player played the same scratchy tunes. There were no windows, there was nothing to look at. Quite often we were the only people there. There were more interesting places to drink, to spend time, but Benito's, even by Tangier's standards, was ridiculously cheap, and Orford, I knew, had to be careful with every penny. God knows what he lived on. He never ate out. He took his meals at Señor Adolfo's, in the small crowded kitchen, with the fatima and Adolfo and Adolfo's boyfriend and Adolfo's mother and occasionally, too, a whore who was down on her luck. A canary chirped in a cage on one wall. A cuckoo clock adorned another. A window looked out on a patch of garden where tethered chickens pecked the hard earth. When the front door buzzed it rang in the kitchen, creating an instant hullabaloo, the canary fluttering, Adolfo springing nervously to his feet. The air was always steamy, potatoes on the boil. Orford ate there silently, rarely saying a word. He ate what was put in front of him, with a polite nod of his head. He had no option. It was what he could afford. His only indulgence was to go to Spain once a month, where he went to see a friend. But it wasn't just the money, why we drank at Benito's, hidden away from café life, the promenading, the faces, the gossip and news. Orford felt himself a failure. He didn't like to be on view.

I asked Orford one evening, when we were sitting in Benito's, had he noticed that our two patrons bore the names of the century's greatest fascists. Orford laughed. He was delighted. 'I think I'll put that in my play,' he said. Orford was only recently a writer. He was beginning with a play. He hoped to emulate the style of Noel Coward, whose work he adored. Noel Coward was his idol. Noel Coward was 'The Master', the beacon to follow. Orford's play was set in a grand English country house, the home of a titled family, and in the first act the debutante daughter gave birth to a black child. Orford wasn't sure what happened after that, in the next two acts. He hadn't worked that out yet. 'Don't worry,' he said, 'it'll write itself. All I need is the momentum.' Meanwhile, he was 'blocking in', as he put it, the first act. He showed me his first pages. 'I know, I know,' he said, 'I can't do dialogue, but don't you think the structure is fine?' I read. Orford chuckled with evil delight. 'Oh, I can just see their faces,' he said. Whose faces? The debutante's titled parents? The stunned audience in a London theatre? I bent over Orford's pages, delaying the moment when I would have to look up. I didn't know what to say.

We would collaborate. I, as a published writer (one short story, an accepted but yet-to-be-published first novel), would handle the dialogue. Orford would furnish the correct nuances of upper-class English life. Together we would evolve the plot, heedful of the example of 'The Master'. Orford was very excited. There was a lot to discuss. We sat in Madame Porte's salon de thé, where the old French of Tangier passed their afternoons, with its potted palms and white-aproned waitresses and trays of delicate patisserie. Classical music played softly through hidden speakers. I ordered coffee, Orford, fearful of his heart, tea. We selected our cakes. We talked. We laughed. We concocted the wildest turns. Orford's hands trembled, his whole face trembled. His usually pale cheeks flushed red. We scribbled notes, characters' names. I knew it would never happen, I think we both knew that, but it didn't matter. That wasn't the important thing. When the bill came Orford attempted to pay but I wouldn't allow it. 'It's all right, Orford,' I said. 'You can pay me back when you're rich.'

'We'll both be rich,' Orford said.

The following afternoon Orford suggested, for the first time, that I might like to meet one of his friends. We set off together to see Miss Mitchell.

I have said that Orford seemed to have few friends, and certainly no-one ever came to visit him in his room at Señor Adolfo's, but there were three or four. In time I was to meet them all, those English widows and spinsters of Orford's generation. One painted. Another wrote teenage romances for a British publisher. A third tended her garden. They all kept busy. They filled their days. They gossiped. They knew all the news. They rushed about the markets with their straw shopping bags, strident and boisterous. They had lived in Tangier for years, they knew it backwards. But why were they there? Some sexual proclivity? Lack of funds? Did they pine for England, dream of one day returning? I didn't ask, I felt it too rude to ask, and if I seemed to see in their busy eyes the sadness of exile, was it really there, or did I force it upon them for my own needs? They were strange ladies, noisy, leathery with sun. And Miss Mitchell – Gladys – was the strangest.

Miss Mitchell's life was dogs and cats. Dogs and cats were her whole life. When Orford unlatched the gate to her garden, dogs flew at us from all directions, yelping and barking, mongrels, mutts, curs, dogs of every shape and size, a huge brown boxer, a torn-eared Alsatian. I was terrified. I didn't dare move. I couldn't even speak. Then Miss Mitchell appeared, running from the house, waving a stick. 'Oh, stop it, dogs!' she cried. 'Stop it at once! Can't you see they're friends?'

She led us to the house, swiping with the stick, a small woman, harried, exhausted, but with a kind face, a kind English face. She could have been a librarian, a lady serving in a village shop. 'Shoo!' she cried.

'Go away, dogs! Not now!' Orford walked stiffly, holding carefully the box of cakes he had brought for our afternoon tea. The garden was a wasteland, a few tattered shrubs, the ground everywhere dug up. Chickens scuffled in a wire pen. A cockatoo hopped on a chain. The house was old, dilapidated, the wooden walls brown with dust. We came in through the kitchen. I thought I was going to be sick. It was the smell, a rank airless stench of animals that filled the house like a plague. It was everywhere. It was in the furniture. It was in the walls. I could feel it in my eyes. 'I know, I know,' Orford said to me softly. 'You get used to it.'

'I'll be with you in a minute,' Miss Mitchell said. 'I just have to feed the cats.'

There were twenty of them, twenty and more, on every horizontal surface in the kitchen; on the table, the shelves, the cupboards, the floor. Miss Mitchell put a huge black kettle on to boil. It was like a signal. The cats began to prowl, pushing at one another, pushing at her. She tore up loaves of bread. The cats became more insistent, pushing harder, growling. When she began to open tins of sardines they leapt at her hands. Miss Mitchell spun this way and that, fending them off with her elbows. It was like some maddened choreography. She mashed the bread and sardines with her fingers, dolloped it out into twenty tins, poured on hot water. The cats were now in a frenzy. She barely had time to stand back. The cats flew. It was all over in less than a minute. Miss Mitchell rubbed a hand over her eyes. She stood like that for what seemed a long time. Then she took a deep breath. 'The tea,' she said. 'The tea.'

I sat with Orford in the sitting room. The smell here was even worse. I was certain I was going to be sick. But it was more than just the smell. It was the bare floorboards, the walls as brown with dust as those outside, the scratched and filthy doors. And more than that. Everywhere, on the walls, on the mantelpiece over the empty fireplace, on the window ledge, on the rickety table in the middle of the room, on the floor, were china dogs, plastic cats, saccharine rhymes to 'Dear Doggie' and 'Darling Pussy' on hung-up tea towels, yellowing calendars with collies and black and white terriers, postcards, cheap paintings; a Woolworths of cloying pet-lover's bric-à-brac. In the poverty of the room it was nauseous and heartbreaking. 'Poor soul,' said Orford. 'She's got no money. Everything goes on those stupid beasts. That's why I always bring these cakes when I come. They're probably the only thing she'll eat all day,' he looked quickly at the kitchen, 'which she'll try to give to *them*, if I don't watch her.'

Miss Mitchell brought in the tea, three cracked cups on a tin tray. Orford opened the box of cakes. I shook my head, no, not for me. I couldn't eat anything. I couldn't even touch my tea. The idea of eating anything here, in this smell, was unthinkable. I looked at Miss Mitchell in her torn cardigan and her dirty cotton dress and her toes pushing out of her shoes – old cracked shoes with the laces gone – and I tried to smile as she sighed and said what a bother it was now that Harold, that was the boxer, could open the bedroom door, which is where she had to put him because he fought with the Alsatian, and two other dogs had to be locked up too, more fighters, in separate rooms, and it was God's own business to remember who was where and who'd been fed and exercised and who hadn't, and yesterday the neighbourhood boys had brought her another dog, poor little thing, they'd found it abandoned. 'Just thrown away!' Miss Mitchell cried, her eyes flaring with outrage. She was on the brink of tears. 'Well, they always know they can bring them here,' she said. 'I'll look after them.'

'Come on, Gladys,' Orford said. 'Eat your cakes, there's a dear.'

She would die. She would die of exhaustion. She would starve to death. In my room at Señor Adolfo's I stared at my typewriter. The front door buzzed, the whores tapped, the canary in the kitchen fluttered in its cage. Orford, in his room, scribbled his country house play. I stared at my typewriter. I could see it all. I could see it exactly. It could be happening now, this very minute. Her heart would give out. She would fall to the floor. The cats would prowl over her body, pushing and growling. The dogs would howl to be fed. They would break out of their rooms, maddened with hunger. They would savage her. They would tear her to pieces. No-one would miss her. Days would pass. And what was left would be found by Orford, poor Orford, come to call, with his kindness, with his box of cakes.

I had arrived in Tangier in January, that month of rains, and now it was April. The days were sunny, and each day hotter than the one before. The heats of high summer, of August, were already in the wings. I spent less and less time in my room. My window was on the wrong side for the sun. On even the brightest days it barely penetrated. There was always a feeling of damp. The view of palm trees and blue sky was like a taunt. I felt constrained. There seemed nowhere to move. The table I sat at, read at, wrote at was less than a pace from the bed. A bulky wardrobe loomed from the opposite wall. Where before I had spent each morning there, now I went out. I sat in the cafés, drinking *café con leche*, smoking. I watched the passing faces, the locals, the regulars, the tourists. I walked. I made friends: a Canadian, a New Yorker, a fellow Australian. In a market I bargained for and bought a rug, and then wondered why. Where would I put it? It lay rolled up on top of the wardrobe, its wonderful colours hidden away, bound up with string. I seemed to see less and less of Orford, too. I lived in dread of it, but there was no talk of our play. When we sat in Benito's together, we sat mostly in silence, listening to those scratchy tunes. Passing Orford's door each morning I began to notice what I hadn't before, or had chosen not to; each morning an empty bottle of wine. 'Si, si,' said Señor Adolfo, sadly shaking his head. '*Barrachio.*'

Was it time to leave, to move on? Should I return to London? I sat in a terraced garden overlooking the Straits. Boats like toys moved to and fro, tracing white wakes in the blue water. The sun shone down. The air was as clear as glass. I could see Spanish roads, rooftops, a village square. I thought of the bookshops in Charing Cross Road, the cinemas in Leicester Square, the solid reassurance of the Sunday papers,

walking through the National Gallery, the Picassos in the
Tate. I sipped my mint tea. I lit another cigarette. Moroccan
music droned in the afternoon. Or should I go somewhere
new, Paris, Finland, Berlin?

No, I hadn't finished with Tangier. I loved it. It was so easy.
It was still so endlessly different. I loved the Socco Grande and
the Socco Chico, the crowded narrow streets, the smells, the
cake seller with his tray buzzing with bees. A little man sold
scissors. 'Very good, cheap,' he cried, clicking them over his
head. I ate chicken and couscous in Moroccan restaurants
tucked away in the medina, finished each meal with a wedge of
watermelon, went somewhere else for coffee, to sit, to talk. I
walked on the wide beaches. I sat in gardens. I strode along
dusty roads in the hills. There was a man who sold hedgehogs.
When you asked to see one he showed you an empty hand.
Then – a wink, a smile – a hedgehog appeared, crawled out
from the wide sleeve of his jellaba.

I sold another short story, my second. Fifty pounds minus
my agent's commission in London was nothing at all; here I
felt splendidly rich. I celebrated in a French restaurant. I
bought a silk shirt, goatskin sandals, had my hair cut, had my
photograph taken in the Socco Grande against a backdrop of
veiled fatimas and rusty buses and rushing boys. I planned a
trip to Casablanca and Marrakesh.

On the ferry from Gibraltar a Moroccan in a business suit
engaged me in conversation. We stood together on the deck,
the bare hills of Africa across the water aged and golden in
afternoon sun. He smiled. He offered me a cigarette. He asked
where I lived in Tangier, how long had I been there, how
much longer did I plan to stay. I had bought whisky and cigars
in Gibraltar, magazines and books, and I felt expansive. I was
an international traveller. I knew the ways of the world. I told
him. I told him what I did. 'I will come to visit you,' he said,
smiling closer, revealing a gold tooth, and I realized at last that
he was making overtures, that he was propositioning me, that
his were the words of homosexual courtship.

'I'm sorry,' I said. 'That's not possible. I am going back to

London tomorrow. I have a girlfriend there,' I said, and walked away, stood somewhere else on the deck, and I felt the danger, my foolishness and vulnerability, but how thrilling it was, too, to have this happen on the deck of a ship, with the brown hills of Africa running beside.

Tangier was full of danger of one sort or another – drugs, the police, robbery, violence; you heard stories all the time – but the greatest danger was something else. I perceived it and acknowledged it. I saw it in those Americans and Englishmen who had lived there for years, the painters, the writers, those who did nothing special or nothing at all but made themselves equally busy, the exiles, the expatriates, the foreign colony. Tangier was so easy. It was so uncomplicated. It was so cheap. It spoilt you for anywhere else. That was the greatest danger. It made you unfit for the rest of the world. Stay one day too long, you felt, and you were here for life.

I would miss it. I would miss the fatimas, the beggars, the jostling narrow streets, the smells, the dust, the noise, the endless strangeness and the wonder of being in its midst. I would never forget it. I would leave. I would go to Paris and Finland and Berlin. Of course I would leave. But not yet. Not yet.

Orford asked a favour. His bank had made a mess-up some-where. Nothing really, but a bother. Be sorted out in a week. Meanwhile, he said, he was a trifle stretched for funds. I took out my wallet. 'No, no, dear boy,' he said. 'I can manage. I'll get by. Very kind of you, though. No, no, what I wanted to ask you was something else.'

We sat in Benito's: the usual white wine, the usual *tapas*, the same scratchy tunes on the old record player. I hadn't seen Orford for a week. He looked terrible. His cheeks were drawn and grained with white stubble. His hands seemed to tremble even more than usual. His eyes were watery and pink.

'My friend in Spain is expecting me,' he said, 'and I'm afraid I can't get over right now. Got myself into a bit of a state, as you can see.' He smiled weakly, 'I wondered if you, if you're going across . . .'

'Well, I was thinking of going tomorrow,' I said.

'She lives in La Linea,' Orford said. 'You take the bus from Algeciras. Drops you right at the door. Very easy. You won't have any trouble finding it.'

'All right,' I said. 'Sure.'

'Oh, wonderful, wonderful,' Orford said. He seemed to brighten up at once. 'I'll write you a letter. Do it as soon as we get back. You can stay the night, which is what I always do. She'll give you dinner, too. She'll be delighted. Doesn't see enough people. Hardly sees anyone, actually. Lives with her mother, which is a bit of a problem. It's all a bit sad. A lovely woman. Russian. Very intelligent. Married an Englishman, just after the war.' Orford shook his head. 'Terrible mistake. Beastly fellow. Met him in Berlin. Well, you know, it was either that or go back to Russia, you know how it was in those days. Anyhow, he's dead. Died two years ago. Can't say I'm sorry, either. A ruffian. Made Sophie's life hell.'

Orford reached for his glass. I put some money on the counter for two more.

'Very good of you,' Orford said. 'I'll write that letter at once.' He drank his wine and then he turned to me, his watery eyes full of apology. 'I'm putting you out, aren't I?' he said.

'Nonsense,' I said. 'Not at all. I like meeting new people. It'll be interesting.'

I stepped from the street through the front door into a court-yard open to the sky. It was late afternoon, five o'clock, after five. I stepped into a sound of birds. I had introduced myself. Now I handed over Orford's letter. Sophie put it in her pocket. 'I will read it later,' she said. 'Dear Orford. He telephoned me this morning. Is he all right? I know, I know, the drinking, always the drinking. Come, we will go upstairs. That is where I sit. We will talk there.'

A wooden staircase led up to the floor above. There was a

balcony. I walked up behind Sophie. Birds darted past, swooping to the ground and up again, in and out of the open sky. They darted in black flashes, in endless flight. 'Oh, the swallows,' Sophie said. 'What a nuisance they are. It is impossible to be rid of them.'

'They're beautiful,' I said.

'Do you think so?' Sophie said, turning on the stairs to look at me.

Then a voice called out. 'Sophia?' I heard. 'Sophia?' We were almost at the balcony.

'Come,' Sophie said to me. She stood by an open doorway.

'Mother,' she said, 'this is a friend of Orford's. From Tangier. He has come to visit.'

She was tiny, like a ceramic doll, all pink and white. This was her bedroom. She lay on the bed in a dressing gown, propped up on pillows. Her bare feet were the smallest I had ever seen. They were perfect, like china. An open book lay face down on her lap. Her eyes were blue, like the sky above the courtyard. They seemed to hold all the life that she had. 'She speaks mostly Russian,' Sophie said to me. 'Do you speak Russian? No?' To her mother she said: 'Your supper will come soon. It is still early. I will come back then.' I smiled politely. The blue eyes smiled back.

I had brought a bottle of whisky as a gift. 'Do we need ice?' Sophie said. 'Water is enough? My husband always drank with soda. The English way.' She made a face. 'Thank you,' she said, accepting a cigarette. 'Ah, this is pleasant.' We sat in a large room with windows onto the courtyard. There was a piano, a table set with chairs half hidden by a screen, dark paintings in heavy frames on the walls: landscapes, stern faces, glowing globes of fruit. Books lay about, magazines. There were flowers in vases, plants in pots. The light, despite the windows, was somehow European. The whole feeling of the room was European; cluttered, lived-in, lace, velvet, turned in on itself. Sophie crossed her legs, tilted up her chin to blow away smoke. 'Tell me,' she said. 'Tell me about the world.'

She was Orford's age, of Orford's generation, and in her

face, under the age, there was that classical structure of character; the high cheekbones, the brow. But her eyes were otherwise. They were too quick, too nervous. There was something beseeching about them. They seemed to plead. We talked. We talked, first, about Tangier, about Orford. Sophie sat forward on her seat, interested in everything I said, her eyes – those beseeching eyes – studying my face. She lit another cigarette. Then we heard her mother calling, 'Sophia? Sophia?' Sophie stood up at once. 'Take another drink,' she said. 'Please.'

This happened four times. The windows grew dark. The swallows fell silent at last. The paintings on the walls were like rectangular holes. I poured another whisky. I could hear Sophie talking to her mother, footsteps, doors, hurrying sounds. I felt like an eavesdropper, alone in that European room. Then Sophie came back with an omelette, an opened bottle of wine. She pulled up a small table. We ate.

She wanted to know everything, where I had been, where I was going. She was interested in everything. It grew late. It was after midnight. Sophie didn't look in the least tired, if anything she seemed more animated. She crossed and recrossed her legs. She lit yet another cigarette. She leaned forward. She perched on her seat, her eyes on mine, endlessly questioning. She wanted more. She would listen all night. I told her about the books I liked, the writers. 'Oh, books, books,' she said. 'What are books? I have books.' Her arms swept across the room. 'Books are not enough.'

She poured another glass of wine, the end of the bottle. She looked down. When she spoke again, her voice was one I had not heard before, a low voice, filled with bitterness. 'Oh, this Spain, this wretched Spain,' she said. 'How I hate it. How I long to go. But how? Where?'

I shook my head. 'It must be very difficult with an invalid mother,' I said.

'Invalid?' Sophie said. She spat out the word. 'She is not an invalid. She is worse than an invalid. You thought her nice? You thought her a pleasant old woman? She is a monster. She

lies on that bed. She watches who comes into the house. She knows everything. There is nothing wrong with her. She is not ill. She can walk like you and I. There is nothing wrong with her legs.'
Sophie stared at me. Her eyes were like running water, except there were no tears. Her checks were dry.
'When I married that man she took to her bed,' she said. 'That was eighteen years ago. For eighteen years she has lain on my throat.'
She stood up. She flung an arm to the windows, to the black night. 'Those swallows,' she cried. 'Those foolish swallows have more freedom than I. I am buried here. I have no life.'

I slept downstairs, in her guest room. Everything had been thoughtfully prepared; an oil lamp, a chamber pot, an Agatha Christie paperback by the side of the bed. There was an ashtray, a jug of water. I woke early, woken by the swallows. The courtyard was alive with them, with their darting and swooping, their wings, their song. It was very early. There were no other sounds. I sat on the bed fully dressed and read. When I heard footsteps I went outside. Sophie was in the kitchen, in her dressing gown. 'You didn't sleep?' she said.
She offered me breakfast, but I said no, I had better be going, I had a lot to do. I thanked her for her hospitality. I promised to give Orford her best regards. I didn't say good-bye to her mother. The bedroom door was closed.
I caught the bus to Algeciras. I found a place with a jukebox, shelves of cigarettes and spirits and wine displayed like fireworks. I sat down at the counter. I ordered orange juice, coffee, a toasted ham sandwich. It was a new place. Everything was chrome and glass and mirrors. Wherever I looked I saw my face.

Winter

Alison Brackenbury

Were mornings always so dark?

It troubled him sometimes, lying with eyes open to their darkness, that he remembered so little. But the past: that bright small end of the telescope, seemed to him the property of the old: itself a kind of winter. His grandmother had told him – not long before she died – of her dream of the night before. Though arthritis had swollen her legs for years, in the dream she was running round and round a grass field with a girl from her home village she had known at school. Hawthorn trees hung over a dark corner of the field and as her companion ran faster, nearer, she cried to her to be careful, to come away, there was a pond there –

Had the girl fallen in? He could not remember. He was just over thirty; not ready for such returnings.

Young or old, November to March remains; the black hole, the tunnel. You leave home in the dark and return to it. When the alarm clicks softly in the morning the mind says sensibly, 'Get up'; the body whispers, 'Wait till it's light, wait till it's *warm* – '

There was little to fear left for him at work; none of the sudden battles lying in wait for Elizabeth. He thought of her by her full, strange name when he had to think of her as a teacher. In long summer holidays she was Liz again; the hurried housekeeping receded and he came home to find her lunch plates scattered in the sink and her? shadowily asleep under the lopped walnut tree, in the long grass, a magazine spread on her stomach. In the crook of her arm he would see the ginger cat, its stripes a dim amber, its tail tipped with cream, turning its pale golden eyes to him as a stranger, its pupils closing against the light. Then Liz would scuffle up the cat and cross the small lawn, heavy with the sun, smelling of heat and half-dried grass. Her hair was very dark, her skin fair; she reddened quickly, and as quickly, peeled down to whiteness. Every September, like that skin, summer fell from her. She grew pale, she caught endless colds; her school-bag bulged with smudged, unmarked books. 'Almost Christmas,' she kept murmuring grimly, blowing her nose. She was very clear about her work and he rarely discussed it with her; listened instead to intricate and passionate stories, sympathized. Once, not long before they married, he had asked her why she corrected the children's local variations of grammar so confidently, and she replied, staring at him a little suspiciously, 'Because it's wrong.' He had concluded that she needed to be so certain to survive in a school; soldiers don't question; teaching is a battle. Liz, he believed, was a good teacher; she cared for the children, she liked most of them. Her longed-for Christmas began with her arriving home with tins of sweets from some classes and a surprising number of bright cards with single names in them; and messages, often misspelt. Liz was modest about all this, caustic to the end about the spelling.

He did not come out of the morning dark to face thirty resentful children. He did not, in that sense, have to 'face' anyone, running the library of a technical college whose battlegrounds lay below his shabby kingdom on the top floor. He had a deputy some years younger than himself, a large girl who always wore a small, silver cross and, he sometimes feared, prayed for him. She plotted vast recataloguing; she had admitted once to waking up still dreaming of classification numbers. Whether they were eluding her or singing, like angels, behind her alarm clock, she did not say. More dashing were the younger girls, arts graduates with coloured socks who read the gloomiest feminist literature, alternately with *Vogue*, in complete cheerfulness and were collected each night by startlingly young and protective husbands or boyfriends. He found the girls easy to talk to, apart from the odd discussion of pain or pills which froze as he came through the door. There were always books to talk about, a high-lit breathless world they seemed to find neutral, comfortable.

Was this right? He was not sure, least so when he turned round from such talk and found one of the student technicians waiting warily at the counter, waiting for a book, an answer, but clearly unhappy, thrust into a strange country. The students included girls with sharp voices, pale tights and black glossy shoes ('misfits' from private schools turned into half-hearted A-level students) and small sixteen-year-old boys who scrawled addresses from council estates unsteadily on their registration cards and asked each other – not him – how to spell 'mechanical'. This is a divided place, the voices said in him. He could tell now, almost by a glance at someone, what they were studying, in which area they lived, who they would speak to, who they would despise, fear, ignore. The library was always too noisy. Groups of students argued with their friends about politics, the crossword, their equations, their motorbikes. They could ignore the faces staring crossly or tiredly at them from the next table; these were not their friends. Consequently he and the girls wasted a good deal of each day cajoling or shouting at them for quiet. On the bad days they mostly shouted and were left with a dark, sulky silence.

Why did he do this? Liz would have said he was good at it; she overrated him. He was only adequate on committees, and rather bad at figures. If his deputy dreamed of classification, he dreamed of accounts. The auditors had arrived, all the account books were missing. He asked the students where they were and they started singing, brilliant indifferent sound – Then the alarm clicked.

Why then, did he do it? Attempts at answers flared in him, disturbed him. Books are not safe. (The people who pay taxes for them, who think they are comforting or irrelevant, might not pay so easily if they understood them better. He remembered sometimes a large and shabby man sitting quietly in a London library, whom he and his assistants might have served politely, perhaps laughed at in secret: a man named Marx.)

Books have no season, yet go past them in dull morning, before anyone is there and you are suddenly aware of them: they surround you, breathing, the dead wood in them stirs, they wait for you: to come into their own. There is space there, there is a chance, there is another country; but it can be darkened, reduced; it is not neutral. So the programmers and the electronic engineers, the sharpest, most assured of the students, read their manuals, demanded the latest editions, waited to get good jobs: to inherit the earth. The less glossy technicians found the books clumsy tools, which failed to provide the exact specification for their job, the model of engine they had been shown. They fought general studies. 'I'm doing engineering; why make me do a stupid project on population?' He watched them learn cunning, photo-copy whole sections of the *Encyclopedia Britannica*, watched them rush off to their early marriages, their quick children; lost an invoice; learnt that one of the girls was leaving to follow a boyfriend; came home to find that Liz was beginning her third cold of the term.

Only riding lit winter. He had always wanted to ride but had no money for it when he was young. In the village where he came from a rich farmer kept racehorses. They were turned into the field next to his house in spring, skittering round the hillocks, 'wild as wind' people said; they ran away, they bucked the small stable lads on to roads, they were too tall for safety, uncontrollable as fire, and he loved them. He still had no fear of horses on the ground; he would stroke them, talk softly to them, coax bits into their mouths. But he realized quickly that he had no talent at all for riding.

He hoped that he had not left Liz with any illusions on this score, but she had no time to watch him ride and no desire to join him. 'I like cars,' she said. 'Horses have no brakes.' He remembered this when he first cantered round the school on the small bouncing brown horse as it struck off, tossing him sharply up and down, he was convinced he would be flung straight off; snatched at the neck strap, the creaking saddle, swore –

'Mind the children!' cried Rachel, the shrill, kind girl who

taught him and ten wide-eyed infants, 'You won't fall off – '
she stopped laughing, tried to instruct, improve, 'Sit up
straight – sit *down* – '

But how you sat down, as a horse tensed and flung and
swerved, was a mystery of harmony he never grasped, a calm
of body beyond his reach, and consequently he never rode
well.

The first time he went out on the hill, when they plunged
into a canter up a long muddy field (without warning, except a
blurred shout into the wind) he was equally terrified, equally
helpless. As the old horse leapt forward, both stirrups were
snatched from his feet and as the chestnut head strained and
tossed after the rest, as mud from the horses in front smacked
against his cheek and the air beat like a blind wave at his eyes,
he saw the ground, heavy, torn, so far (the old horse was tall),
so perilously near and hard. He hung to the reins as his last
hope, he called nonsense to the indifferent, sweating golden
neck before him, this strength, this madness; this is why Liz
won't ride. Horses can kill you – then he heard the old horse
panting, felt the flanks shudder, the gallop die into a rocking
and dull canter; he pulled his horse up beside the others, rooks
beating up out of the bare trees ahead and he was held in a
harsh and hot exultation. This was the world he had forgotten;
the high winter light still spinning in the hill's trees, the
glint of the reservoir as they filed down the narrow path,
water springing and dodging the stones. Every evening after
riding he slept like a child, peaceful, filled with cold and
exhaustion.

To his surprise, Liz did not seem to mind him disappearing
every Sunday afternoon. She said she had things to do. There
was little evidence of her activities, except a brief tangle with
knitting, and he suspected that she spent the two hours asleep
somewhere, with her cat. But why not? He was touched by
the thought of her, lost in the grey deep haze which is afternoon sleep in the suburbs, under constant threat of harsh
ice-cream music or a child's shout . . . and beside her, the
cat, closed tight as a squirrel, nose soft in the deep amber of
its tail.

Perhaps it was this practised separation that made Liz insist he went alone to the party.

'It will be awful,' she said, blowing her nose. 'You're the unlucky one having to go. All the grey suits will be there.' He denied this, smiling. He had once told Liz that everyone who worked at the college for any time ended up wearing the same kind of grey suit, that these could find their way to the Tech. in the mornings without their owners, like a procession of elephants; that one day he would wear one.

'And then,' Liz persisted, 'the Wife – '

Most people at the college did not like each other enough to welcome parties. The Wife (Liz's unloving name) overruled this. She had a house to warm, that was enough. She was young, glinting with assurance and an extraordinary collection of rings. Some were the hard stones, sea's jade, cold turquoises. But once he had turned to speak to her and found himself staring into blurring, blue depths: an opal: unchanging breath without heat, like a kiss without love, an unlucky stone.

'Be good,' Liz said, suddenly, irrelevantly, as he was leaving. The cat moved closer to her feet.

The house did not need warming; it was already too full. He talked half-heartedly to someone about their car, wandered off pretending to look for a drink; was 'rescued' by the host whom he did not know well (did anyone? did the Wife?) He started talking about learning to ride with the ten competent children. This was an unexpected success in making his host laugh – a mistake. The Wife appeared.

'What are you talking about? Riding? I wouldn't have thought – ' A hand rose; he saw again that cold smoke of blue light over one finger. 'Tom, will you see to the drink? Well, if you ride, you must meet – ' She called over her shoulder; he hardly caught the name.

The girl did not hurry. She had a long blue dress, thin, very brown shoulders. She smiled at him. She did not seem afraid of the Wife.

'We were at college together. She used to try to organize me then. You ought to give up, Anna.'

The Wife, who, thanks to Liz, he had never thought of by name, said nothing but smiled, almost tenderly; lifted her other hand. Black of jet, fretted ivory, placed them: I have arranged you: five minutes. She turned, to stir her party.

He thought five minutes would be plenty. It was clear, far too quickly, that the girl rode very well. She kept her own horse.

'It bankrupts me. Do you have one?'

'I ride at a riding school,' he said. 'But' (he had hardly thought about this) 'I should like to.'

She said it was much easier to ride one horse all the time. You came to know it, trusted it. Her eyes glinted grey. She stood very straight, looked at him directly, did not fidget. She had brown hair slipping forward over her thin forehead, but did not push it back. She rode cross-country courses, 'You have to know a horse for that, the fences are so big.' And at the thought of the raw ditches and fixed timbers, that terrible rush of air and suspense, he, who had swerved away from low heaps of beech twigs in the quiet woods, gave up all attempts to go along with this.

'I've looked at those courses. I don't think I could ever ride them.'

The contempt he expected did not come. She accepted, much as a horse takes a sudden obstacle in a stride. In the idiocy of the thought he recognized that bright blurring of sight and sense which means wine has reached your head. Whose voice, so clearly, 'Yes, too late when you make a mistake. I make bad ones. I once gave up riding for a year – I broke my wrist.'

She lifted her hand, bare of rings; and he saw the slight thickening, the stiffness. He saw too the blue veins that flare on the wrist before they are spread into the hand: quick, generous.

'But you like riding outside? Yes? I don't like indoor riding. It's cramped.'

'It's the space outside,' he said, hearing echoes through his own voice, 'the light.'

'Yes.'

'And do you hunt?'

She looked at him. Too closely. It is not what you say.

'I did at one time. You can't stop them out there, you just hang on – sit – and they go mad. I liked that. But I gave it up.'

He knew he ought to say something, head off. But his reactions were slower than hers. He found himself staring at a spray of huge silk flowers on Anna's mantelpiece, impossible colours; peacock blue, the air's gold.

And not facing her, sensing her smile, he heard her say, too direct, too close, 'I was right to say that. You don't like hunting people.'

'Not quite,' he said carefully, watching her face, her eyes. 'I like some of the people who hunt. But to chase something, for miles, even though it kills – '

'Yes, yes.'

Her long mouth relaxed; her smile kept no mockery. She leaned against the mantelpiece, her elbow sharp and small by the theatrical, scentless flowers and began to talk softly, easily: a conversation warm and brief as the wine in his head, odd, too fast, a sharpening of smoky air. It is not what, but how tenderly, you speak.

She worked in computing; she sorted out after-sales problems for customers; she travelled; it paid well, so, the horse. She spoke of her house on the outskirts of a Midland city.

'And you – ?'

A flash of perfume: the Wife. How ruthless, how perfect was her sense for people. This is going on too long. She was no longer a joke. For a moment he hated her.

'You must come and meet – '

'No, Anna, I must go now. You remember, I said I would have to get back.'

To whom? he wondered at once, and then he knew, it did not matter; she does not wear rings; she is free. She had gone with Anna, still arguing. He went to get a drink. The kitchen was hot with people, it took a long time; she would, he told himself firmly several times, be gone.

She was in the hall. In trousers, with a duffel coat and bag, she looked younger. She took two quick steps forward.

'Don't forget, you can ring me if you ever come that way. I'm in the phone book.' She smiled, shook back her hair. 'I can always borrow a horse.'

Light as air. Had anyone told her about Elizabeth? Then Anna was past him, calling her husband to come and say goodbye. As the three moved together to the door he realized that she would throw his wife's name back at him, as she had his questions; that was for him to decide; she was ruthless, remote as Anna, but alone.

Out of her pocket, just missing Tom's feet, the scarf uncurled.

'How were the grey suits?' Liz sighed out of sleep. He seemed to smell alcohol on her. He must have drunk more than he thought.

'Talking about cars,' he said carefully. 'Some of Anna's college friends were there.'

'Awful, awful – Poor love – ' said Liz softly beside him, heavier than usual? perfectly deceived.

(For it is that easy. A scarf, folded small. A letter. The address is in the phone book which the library has. Books cease to be neutral as soon as a hand touches them. He gets up before Liz every morning; he can rummage through it all, the catalogues, the teachers' monthly news-sheet, his mother's weekly letter, the bills. The scarf was silk, not lime, or blue-green of seas but green as grass; the grass Liz lies in all summer. This is why hands tremble, why vows are made, why children are taught: a green scarf for a cold night, generous and simple as the sun.)

But next day his head ached. Nothing was clear. He knocked a wineglass left on the draining board into the sink, where it lay in white shivers of ice.

'What was it doing there, anyway? Were you drinking last
night?'

Liz only smiled, turned away. She was in an odd mood.

He had the young horse, Toby. He had last ridden him in the
summer when Toby displayed two passions: eating and standing still. Brought out of his dark box he lunged hopefully at
the owner's tub-bound daffodils. But dragged away he
bucked, with a sharp rattle of feet on the yard.

'He's off again,' the young stable girls cried. 'He bucked
someone off three times this morning – He's mad today – '

He didn't believe them. They teased everyone; when the
customers stopped amusing them they chased each other
round the yard with steaming forkfuls of muck. But as soon as
the horses turned out into the road he knew they were right.
Toby tried to canter, whipping away from him, he was a thin,
tall horse, foxy dark. He whirled sideways from white gate-
posts, plunged at junctions towards cars whose drivers – faces
shining with fury and fear – braked just in time. Hunched in
the narrow saddle, he was sweating. He's like a racehorse. I
can't ride him like this.

As they cantered up the bare hillside, a pony started thrust-
ing through from the back; a child screamed. He felt Toby
shoot forward to bolt, but there were two hunters pounding
heavily in front; nowhere for them to go. Then the tense back
exploded upwards and he was over the warm shoulder, tumbling down – on the ground. There were horses coming up
behind: half the ride. Seeing himself for a blink of a second
from above, like a jockey, fallen at a fence, he rolled up; as he
shielded his eyes he saw the first belly and hooves rise dark
over him, one hoof grazing the shoulder of his jacket. He hid
his eyes; he heard more horses passing over, swerving close.
Then the ground stopped shaking and he opened his eyes to
see them all, stopped, looking very small and bright, calling,
'Are you all right?'

★

'Are you really all right?' Liz stared at him, turning still paler.

'Yes,' he said, trying not to think about the dark feet, the last dazzle of light before he shut his eyes. Liz produced some wine. This was unexpected; she was normally a careful house-keeper, and did not buy such things. 'To soften the shock', she said.

Some time later she told him she was pregnant.

It is not what you say. You must be very careful. She is not looking at you, she is staring at the wine which is shaking softly in the glass and whatever you say now she will remember; for she has an almost perfect memory, not like you.

'Are you pleased?' she said.

'Yes,' he said. And like exhaustion, relief overtook him, for it was true: you hit the ground, you think, I didn't mean to be here, it was a mistake, but I took the risk and it was not as hard as it might have been: yes.

(And it will be easier now; there will be less time to ask questions; you will have something to talk about to the men who care about cars; they have children too. Your deputy will be pleased; she'll marry one day, suddenly, have her first child quickly. You had never realized that before. You will under-stand more now, you will be in tune with things. You will be less selfish.)

He kissed Liz slowly. The cat yawned, a pink cave in drowsy fur. She laughed.

He said he had already decided to give up riding; it cost too much and the fall had decided it.

'No – ' she protested.

'Yes,' he said.

The postman's bicycle wheels whirred along the pavement, like rain. The mornings were lighter now; light enough to see the letter lying on the green carpet. The writing was clear, lightly angled, just as he had imagined it. Hers.

He could not breathe for a moment. His eyes swam. Then

he bent down and saw that it was addressed to Mrs Falk, who had their number, but in the next road.

(It could not have been hers. Yes, he had looked up her address in the directory, he had stared at it for a long time until a boy with red hair had come to ask him for a book on transducers. He had written no letter. Yes, she had dropped the scarf, but she had turned and scooped it up immediately – would someone so quick miss that? had turned without a look and was gone into the dark.)

I can borrow you a horse.

He went into the kitchen. Upstairs he could hear Liz talking to the cat in the sunlit bedroom, easing herself off the bed, pattering stiffly to the bathroom. He went to the back door and looked out.

For the sweet rhythm of the seasons is not in us, or only briefly. We choose; we suffer. We cannot quite forget in the dark. A girl with thin brown shoulders: quick and beautiful as light. I shall not write.

Do not dare say, however strangely, I did not love her.

He looked out to the great ash tree, on his neighbour's ground. The sky he had thought soft hung silver over it, the depths metallic. The bark glowed brilliant; steady. The pool of leaves at its foot did not reflect just the sun; or yet, the stir of tender leaf. The tree flares into still air, every twig, every bud quick and unconsumed, aflame: with frost.

The Human Sacrifice
Glyn Hughes

My Aunt Ida used to sit in a small room crammed with mirrors, mahogany furniture and sea pictures. She was fat and lodged herself in a chocolate-brown upright chair. One mirror was angled over the mantelpiece, one above the sideboard opposite, three hinged in a triptych, one above a glass case full of china, and one in the budgie's cage. They gave her views outside in all directions. She might seem to be taking no interest in them – she picked at her apron, watched wrestling on TV, nagged the dog, the budgie, her husband or myself her bored nephew, or asked my mother direct questions that she was too genteel to answer. But suddenly in mid sentence Aunt Ida would become distracted, and as she moved slightly to adjust her view the floor and furniture shook, the bell in the budgie's cage rang, the mirrors rippled with light and their bevelled edges splattered rainbows. She reminded me of a fat trout, mouth open, lodged in her shadow eddy amongst glittering mirrors as in a rush of shining water, and waiting for food to drift towards her.

On the opposite side of the road was a telephone box, on which the life of the village focused. This was the sluice through which Aunt Ida's information poured. 'There's that Mrs Becket again! That's the sixth time she's been a-phoning since yesterday tea. She never lets on.' Aunt Ida whispered, '*It's her husband. They say he was beneath all that women's underwear that was stolen.*' Ida never said anything good about anyone. Never. For instance the newsagent nearby used every day to polish the telephone box, he even carpeted and hoovered it! It was not his duty, but if he missed, Aunt Ida complained.

The road sped in a straight line over the flat land, which ICI had smashed and filled with flaming retorts, like the experiment of a mad giant apothecary; there the heavy sky was tucked over the edges of the countryside and the horizon appeared bent under the weight of it. This sky seemed to suck one up and a number of medieval mystics were born here; the kind of people who crawled to Rome on their hands and knees, and ate diets of thistles. One was tempted in this district either to float off into madness, or to find a dark hole in which to cringe in fear. The nearby town actually fell into a hole. This was because of the salt, which was dissolved and pumped out of the ground, leaving a cavity under the earth.

When my aunt moved into her cottage there had merely been salt carts and herds of cattle rambling by, but by degrees the road had widened and now lorries thundered through. Aunt Ida hated them shaking and darkening her house. It was really envy because they came and went over the horizon, not caring a damn for anyone, whilst Aunt Ida never went anywhere, though once when I was six she took me to the pictures. She wrapped herself in a mackintosh cape of white rubber in case it rained, and she looked like a covered railway truck moving up the street. I stood between her knees at the front of the bus, kissing the window and shifting to steam up fresh places with my breath. 'Is he over six?' the conductor asked suspiciously. Aunt Ida was getting indignant when I said, innocent and angelic, 'I'm seven.' I'm glad I said it because it's the only time I've seen Aunt Ida lost for words.

The cinema was like a round tin half-buried sideways in the ground. There was no sign of anything being shown and the proprietor was mowing his lawn next door. He had been to school with Aunt Ida and he said that his cinema had been closed for five years, which I knew from having passed by before. After that I don't think she ever went further than the nearby Co-op, until she had to visit her gentle husband in hospital when he was dying of throat cancer.

Uncle Billy, on the other hand, had two bicycles to wander about on. One was a rusty old thing caked with salt and potash, on which he cycled to work at ICI. He would get up at six o'clock in the morning alone, and I would hear him coughing over his first cigarette while he raked out the fire. It took him so long, that once I got up to see what he was doing. In his blue, pressed boiler suit, he was on his knees before sheets of newspapers laid over the tiles, polished brass and black leading of Aunt Ida's fetish, the fireplace. (Most of the work at Aunt Ida's cottage seemed to be done on hands and knees – mopping the floor, feeding the dog and stopping the draughts.) Whilst the kettle boiled on the fresh coal and sticks, Uncle Billy gave me a lesson on doing a job tidily – he believed that he was giving me tips for my future marriage. Before 1914 he had been a foot-boy at the Manor, opening gates and cleaning shoes. At the age of sixteen he was an able-seaman on a destroyer in the Bosphorus; devious battles with Turks, Greeks, Russians and Germans. Uncle Billy never fathomed out which side he was on – which, I suppose, taught me a great deal about English diplomacy. After the war he started at ICI and married my Aunt. I used to wonder if in those days she smiled with something other than malice, or whether she was always predatory. Anyway, on this one morning I watched him; he folded the newspapers around the ash from the grate, put aside his Woodbine and ate his breakfast that Aunt Ida had laid for him the night before. The tea leaves in the pot, milk and triangles of thinly sliced bread under crocheted cloths weighed down with beads, two rashers of bacon in the frying pan; and then he tidied up after himself. Then out, waking the silent dawn with his squeaking bike.

His other, his 'best' bicycle, was breathtaking. It was glossy as a bluebottle, hubs and spokes shining; a heavy green Raleigh, ten or fifteen years old. He would take it out only at weekends and bank holidays, if the weather was fine. Other times he kept it in the back bedroom where my mother parked me for weeks on end – her relatives being without children, and she having so many troubles to cope with. Apart from the bicycle my temporary bedroom was filled with superfluous furniture, covered in dust sheets and placed to face the wall. Before I climbed into bed, my aunt made me strain over a

chamber pot, whether I wanted to or not. After I had satisfied
her with some sort of a leak, I had to remain kneeling and say
my prayers. I prayed aloud for my mother and Uncle Billy,
and under my breath for my father because if Aunt heard his
name, she treated me to a sermon on his sins. I tried to leave *her*
out, but she reminded me of it. 'And doesn't Aunt Ida deserve
a word?' she would say, towering over me in a pink, iron
corset. All this kneeling, devotional pissing and praying was
done in front of Uncle's bicycle as if it was an altar. And after
I'd got under the sheets, listening to the rattle of my Aunt
undressing and hearing her making my Uncle piss in the next
room, the sight of the Raleigh bicycle catching the theatrical
light of the street lamp was the last thing I closed my eyes
upon.

I was longing for a sunny weekend when I might actually see
that bike rolling – any sign of a cloud and Uncle Billy changed
his mind. At last one brazenly sunny day he put on the suit
he'd got married in and wheeled out the Raleigh. He might
have been bringing out a sacrificial calf. He dusted it with his
handkerchief and mounted. I rode my own bike between him
and the kerb and we entered the countryside. Aunt, through
her complicated trick of mirrors, watched us go, and the dog
lolled along beside us, happy but amazed.

Row upon row of hedges were scribbled across the countryside like untidy handwriting. The narrow lanes were
fringed with overhanging cow parsley, buttercups, vetch,
honeysuckle, dandelions and hawthorn – the virginal countryside before selective weedkillers, a scented memory of
Eden! I wondered why Uncle Billy didn't take his bike out
more often for he was enjoying himself so much. He didn't
talk a lot. He tried to tell me about the past, but it was as if his
history was a rag stuffed down his throat, choking him.
'Don't trust anyone,' he summed it all up. He was always
pressing that lesson on me – I think he thought that I was a
too-trusting child. You might say that the fate of that genteel
countryside taught the same lesson, too. Felled beech tree
rotting in the salt pans; country houses stripped of their tiles

and looking like the carcases of dead birds; abandoned gardens, labourers' or gamekeepers' cottages, and ornamental gateways stranded amongst the chemical operations – how the countryside had been betrayed.

Our cycle ride wasn't purposeless: we wouldn't have dared to return 'empty-handed'! We were to visit Aunt's sister, to make excuses for my Aunt not having been to Chapel; and then bring back firewood pulled from the bottoms of hedges. The sister was caretaker of the Chapel. It was a plain brick thing, with an entrance for each of the sexes and a lean-to caretaker's cottage. When they all started singing and praying in there they were as mad as hatters: I remember once an ambulance being fetched in mid service when a mild old spinster, who kept a sweet shop, burst a blood vessel singing 'Maker, I come! I come!'

Aunt Ida also enjoyed going off her rocker in chapel – 'Having a good sing' she called it. I saw her bottom every evening in the bedroom, but her tonsils only on Sundays, pink as a wedding as she sang, her bosom heaving in her black clothes. Aunt Ida's excuse for not going to chapel was that she had no-one to take her. The way she put it, it was a cutting insult to those who could have fetched her in a motor car, but the way Uncle Billy said it, it merely sounded sad. He knew that his wife loved sitting in a motor car, watching the countryside unreel outside whilst she complained that her carriage wasn't as grand as it might be.

It took some talking over and I was bored. Those country rooms in summer all had the same atmosphere. The doors were left open to dry up the damp, the flies mingled and landed on sticky flypapers hung from the light bulbs, the dogs and cats yawned and nibbled themselves, there came in a smell of grass, a sound of cows and hens. The quiet, religious life of this countryside so bright outside exuded a drowsy, intoxicating peace, while I was stuck in a boring drone of adult conversation, as if in honey. Eventually the table was laid with spam, tinned fruit and tinned cream. An overgrown orchard surrounded the chapel – fresh apples, pears, gooseberries, plums, damsons and raspberries rotted outside and the plump cows squirted their cream into churns for a factory – but it had recently become demeaning to pick up the fruit and insulting to offer guests anything but 'hygienic' tinned stuff from the Co-op.

Uncle Billy didn't want to stay because he felt uneasy with Chapel folk. He hadn't escaped from home only to walk into another prison of mirrors and mean asides this sunny afternoon! His big labourer's hands twitched restlessly around his Woodbine or over the knees of his dark suit smelling of moth-balls, and soon we were out again, Uncle Billy's Raleigh hubs ticking and humming along the lovely lanes as we kept our eyes skinned for firewood. He showed me wild flowers. Where violets grew, and the secret, only place where there were still primroses. I can remember his smile when he explained 'parson in the pulpit' – the white surpliced stamen of the wild arum, set in its petal. He kept a roll of string under his saddle, to tie up a bundle of sticks generally gathered at the last minute before we got to the house.

A person who goes outdoors, returns glowing with an experience which he knows he cannot convey and he anticipates a sudden restriction and resentment – such as my aunt's, who was a solid block of it, as she squinted in her mirrors, hoping for something to be brought to her and knowing she wouldn't get it. I believe she kept that budgie in a cage in order to have a fellow sufferer. (Uncle Billy by contrast went in for racing pigeons, which he loved to watch fling themselves in a few minutes over the horizon that he himself hadn't crossed since he returned from the war.) We were silent for the last few hundred yards before we reached the house. As Uncle dusted his bike again before he wheeled it into the bedroom, he cleared his throat; meaning, 'the price is going to be high, but it's worth it.'

I was by nature a goer-outer like my Uncle – it grew with my opposition to my education. School, my relatives, everything absorbed out of the air in a northern working-class environment, was teaching me to choose to do the difficult thing in the most difficult way – whatever came naturally had to be cowed and forced into a mould by the sweat of your brow. We even put iron forms upon our pleasures. Bank holiday traffic jams, for instance; most people could find somewhere delightful nearer home, but what they enjoy is not being beaten, is sweating it out. It's like climbing mountains or plumbing the seas, which we Protestants are very good at. I soon spotted that only fools and working-class slaves suffered like this. Clever people followed the *easiest* route. At junior school I had a desk by the window in the sun – where I could watch the rooks and the people passing. I failed every test that might have moved me up into another class and they thought I was a dunce until they shifted me from this sunny desk. Whereupon my natural education of watching things and people seized up. Until I discovered that I could simply step out of doors and nobody could stop me. I'd ask to be 'excused' and then once I'd faced the fatal question 'why go back?' I could not return. One day, two days. I lay on the grass or in the woods, staring up at the sky. I wish now that I'd done it more often, because those are the days that I remember. The others seem to have been wasted; a form of non-life. Because of this, I grew up under my aunt's suspicion. If I was comfortable in her house, she suspected revolution. 'Don't lean your head on the wall, young man! You'll get Brylcreem on it' – even though she knew I didn't wear hair cream.

Despite my hatred of school, I became a schoolmaster. It was a mistake, a temporary illusion that other people who advised me must be right, and quite comparable with my dear Uncle Billy's suffering the chemical works all his life. But one day I met a man scything a field, and the smell of grass, the sunshine, the flowers, the man's satisfaction, made me realize that I'd been telling lies in order to imprison children in school all day. I still haven't gone back. Without ever opening the letters from the education office, I worked on little farms, wrote poetry and Aunt Ida said that was why her hair turned white. (She was going bald as well.) Uncle Billy turned aside her request for his opinion and made a grating noise in his throat. My aunt thought I'd settle down after I married. But I walked out of that, too. Then I married a foreign woman.

Dezzy was from the Mediterranean coast and was used to living out of doors, half-naked all summer, swimming and drinking fresh orange juice daily, sleeping on verandahs, sleeping in the afternoon and singing half the night, weeping shamelessly when unhappiness visited a neighbour, and kissing folks at the drop of a hat. She was dark-skinned, her hair was as black as tar. She was a mystery to me always. She told me that her birth certificate had been burnt in the records office during a military coup and I never found out precisely how old she was – she kept telling me different ages, within a range of ten years. Did she come from North Africa? Spain? Italy? Greece? Turkey? She was so confusing and I never found out. If she was homesick, she fed us with a thin gruel made of lentils, as eaten in villages during the period of Christ's torment, and that was one clue – she was from a Christian country. There were few others. How could I explain to her Aunt Ida's budgie-cage world, where everything was prosaically accounted for? By that time, I had not been to my aunt's and uncle's for years and it would be an embarrassment to turn up now, so I tried to describe it but I failed; in the end I had to take Dezzy for a peep into it.

Everyone watched us arrive. The newsagent came out of the telephone kiosk with his hoover, winding up the flex, smiling, almost bowing. Ida's neighbours – 'Them as never spoke, them with a mucky dustbin', as she called them – brought all their kids into the front garden. The cottage door was unlatched by Uncle Billy, then he retreated shyly, to wash pots and smoke in the back and put food down for a dog too fat and lazy to eat it. Dezzy entered with a kiss ready to fly off her lips and her arms full of little presents, but the atmosphere stopped her dead. The mirrors glittering like sheets of ice in a cave, the fat dog slopped on the hearth rug, and the table ready-laid, as in the chapels and the cottages of my boyhood, with hygienic adulterated food.

On the instant, Aunt Ida complained that I had 'neglected'

her. Next, realizing with satisfaction that she had killed my emotion with that single arrow, she filled the teapot, sat down opposite and looked Dezzy straight in the teeth. 'Are them your own teeth?' she said. The poor girl thought that she must have misunderstood the English language. 'They're nothing but a nuisance is teeth. I got rid of mine as soon as I could. Look'. Aunt Ida took out the upper set and showed them.

Dezzy tried again. As an expression of warmth and good will, she attacked the table and started spreading margarine on the bread. 'What you doing, young lady? Them's been buttered a'ready. We don't all have a fortune in the bank,' Aunt said whilst she leapt to scrape the margarine off again with the back of a knife. 'I suppose you'll have a lot of funny ways where you come from,' she added, tartly.

Dezzy got on fine with Uncle Billy, although his throat was sore so he didn't say much, and as soon as he tried, Aunt Ida interrupted. 'Our Billy does get throats! It's that potash he's been loading into trucks for twenty years. And I never thought he'd stick it out beyond the first week! He was a bit of a rebel, same as me laddo here' (meaning me). Then she added, 'I've got a good husband though, even if I say it as shouldn't. Some haven't been so lucky' – meaning my mother.

Dezzy simply by being herself would have disrupted their lives. She began by putting her gifts of flowers on top of the television set; then she wanted to move the television because it wasn't a good setting for the flowers. In twenty years I hadn't dared touch so much as a plaster peach or a 'good luck from Blackpool' ornament. Dezzy told them to put their dirty dog out of doors, move the budgie's cage from where it overhung the table, shift the sofa to where it would catch the sun, open the windows, eat fresh fruit, wholemeal bread and less fat. Uncle Billy was tickled pink and he said 'yes' to everything. Aunt Ida said 'no' (to put it briefly). What an afternoon: Dezzy called my aunt plain 'Ida', got her in the garden and after an hour's coaxing in the sunshine hung a daisy chain round her neck.

We hardly ever went there again. If we met at my parents'

house, Ida would hardly talk to us. I remember one Saturday afternoon her watching wrestling on television, and confronting Dezzy about it. 'You don't like wrestling, do you?' she said with deadly aim – for my wife had not said a word on the subject. But if you want to know why there's so much violence in newspapers and on TV, you need to understand people like my Aunt Ida, who eat it up, and we discussed wrestling. Somehow it naturally led us to feeding one another with drops of poison all afternoon – complaining about this or that person. Dezzy raged at this slow-drip erosion. Her own family was either infinitely tender or openly angry towards one another and she could not understand our feelings of love or hate remaining unexpressed; or how, for instance, we could fail to telephone one another during long absences.

Through the following years Uncle Billy's sore throat grew worse, it felt to him as though it was full of nails, and he had to go for 'check ups'. One day they sent him to Christie's cancer hospital in Manchester. Even after that we made ourselves believe it was not cancer but a 'growth' that could be cured with painful radiation treatment. Uncle Billy always said he was 'a bit better, thank you' – his speech now no more than a grating noise at the back of his throat. No matter how thin and yellow he became, he was more frightened of staying off work than he was of pain and its treatment. Although a bit of sunshine would have done him good, he never dared step out of doors because his workmates or their wives might say, 'if he's fit to go out he's fit to go to work'. I think the pair suffered most from things like this, and from having to comfort one another during the tedious journeys they made on country bus routes to the hospital. Dezzy wanted Uncle Billy to cease those terrible trips and cure himself by stopping smoking and with a diet of avocado pears and plenty of fresh air, but Ida was indignant. She said that his Woodbines were the only pleasure left to him, and that the only thing he could swallow was pre-digested baby food, so how could he take to them fancy foreign pears?

I remember the last trip that we made to the cottage before

they took Uncle Billy permanently to hospital. The whole landscape seemed by this time to have grown cancerous, pumping up chemicals and burning off the waste in metal pipes spreading more and more everywhere. Indoors was more or less the same; the dog getting fatter and sleepier, the mirrors, a space left because the budgie's cage had been shifted into the back bedroom now that the bird was dead, flies hovering around a yellow flypaper, a kettle hissing upon the fire, a table laid with sliced bread curling at the edges and invisibly spread with margarine, a plate of wobbly compressed meat keeping the shape of its tin, a milk jug covered by a cloth weighed down with tinkling coloured beads, and at Uncle Billy's place were three small tins of Heinz baby food. Aunt Ida told me that Uncle Billy was leaving me his bicycle and his wedding suit in his will and I choked upon saying that I didn't want them.

With a bad conscience I have often wondered since why I could only bear to visit Uncle Billy once in hospital. On that one visit he tried to explain to me the history of my family, the words 'wrong', 'violets' and 'bike' choked in that gurgling sluice at the back of his throat. It seemed to me that, as all religions demand human sacrifice one way or another, so Uncle Billy was a sacrifice to the God who was exploiting our countryside. And I suddenly realized that Aunt Ida in her loneliness wanted me now to take up his sufferings, his role of sacrifice. I could not go to that hospital again, and I felt only a numbed determination about this – as when I used to stay away from school. But perhaps my own choked besieged feelings have ever since been cultivating a cancer deep within me, who knows?

I did not, in the end, get either the bicycle or the suit. And Dezzy never understood how we northerners protected our nerve ends by applying a painful slow burn to them, until eventually they were sealed, and we seemed to be without feelings.

Five and Twenty Ponies
Marshall Walker

The red blur was her sweater behind the frosted glass. Her fist came in and out of focus as it hammered on the pane.

Ben opened the door.

She stumbled in at him like a wounded bird, head down and to the side. Her right hand reached for his neck as her body balled into his arms; the smaller, the safer.

'Daddy. Oh, Daddy, Daddy.'

There were no bruises. The *News of the World* would not have been interested and she wasn't game for the social worker. Not in Glasgow, deprivation city. The social workers had their hands full in Easterhouse, Blackhill, the trouble spots. West End problems were expected to solve themselves. Vague emotional injuries were a middle-class indulgence. Besides, she was too old. In a child of six running away is serious, a symptom. A child of six is innocent, vulnerable, still trails clouds of glory. A girl of eleven, dark, not quite pretty, brown eyes qualified by too much nose, had to be different. Wilful, perverse.

'So cool it, big Daddy,' Ben thought. 'You're the grass on the other side of the street.'

Was age really so important? He still tensed when furniture creaked at night, and dodged into the subway to breathe its furry, damp effluvium, and cried at the end of *A Farewell to Arms*. If at thirty-five he was really somewhere between five and seventeen, what did that do to the social worker's line on an eleven year old who ran away to Daddy? Anyway, Charlotte had been six when the divorce came through. Ben had sung to her nearly every night until he made the break. Maybe the singing had stunted her growth.

Now, the front door of the flat still swinging open in the wind that funnelled up from the close-mouth, she huddled into him.

'Where's Mama?'

Not the Victorian pronunciation, but 'Mama' as in Augusta, Georgia where Ben had found his Annie, or in Atlanta where a mountainous JP had married them on the seventh floor of the County Courthouse. The JP's fee had taken fifteen of their remaining twenty-two dollars, condemning them to a celebration of one whiskey sour each before a squint-eyed manager of the Union Planters' National Bank heard their petition for credit against Ben's first cheque from the State University. After Annie had selected a purple hippo, harlequin pyjamas, and an inflatable chipmunk to sent her new step-daughter in Scotland, there was enough credit left for a phone call to bring Charlotte into the party.

'Hey, how's my old parcel?'

The endearment, backfiring, nearly wrecked the whole thing. Beside him in the booth, Annie was on her third Kleenex and Ben felt the quiver in his own voice. The just deserts of sentimentality. A father who walked out on his child wasn't entitled to be sentimental. It confused the child. He had to be a little formal, a little remote, for her sake. But it wasn't Charlotte he had left, she must know that. Born into a marriage of true impediments, she had come like a consolation prize, an unexpected parcel to be opened, layer by layer. Consolation had not, in the end, been enough to hold him. But he would come back, he would, with his pretty lady from Georgia, and the parcel would love her too.

'How's it going?' Ben said into the telephone.

'Fine.'

'What did you do today, parcel?'

'I was playing in the garden. I got new sandals.'

'Well, listen. Don't get them full of that gravel in the path or it'll hurt your feet. What time is it over there?'

'Almost eight. Mummy says I'm having a bath tonight.'

'Terrific.' Ah, you phoney, she'd catch that false note. 'Bet you fall asleep in five seconds after a day in the garden and a bath.'

'Daddy.'

'Yes, parcel.'

'Daddy, I miss you.' God. Did anyone ever think of telling the child to use a little formality?

'I miss you too, parcel.' Come on, Daddy, come on. Get love along that line. Give her something she can use. 'Listen, you're going to bed in a wee while?'

'Yes, Daddy.'

'Let's sing the song, okay?'

'Okay.' A smile in the voice; she'd got the message. It would need to be soft but very clear if they were to hear each other in duet. Point consonants, easy on sibilants. Pauses between the lines to allow for the time-lag of long-distance.

'Right. I'll start. We'll do the refrain. Ready?'

'Yes, Daddy.'

'Okay. "Five and twenty ponies, Trotting through the dark, Brandy for the parson, Baccy for the clerk, Laces for the lady," ' Ben paused.

' ". . . Laces for the lady," ' his daughter sang.

' "Letters for the spy, And watch the wall, my darling, While the gentlemen go by." ' What would Kipling have thought of this use of his song? Smuggling love into the enemy camp. Be a man, my son.

'Daddy, that was lovely. I've got to go for my bath now.'

'Goodnight, old parcel.'

Annie closed the front door and took Charlotte to the kitchen, hushing the sobs. Ben stood in the hall and wondered what to do next. Did you call your lawyer at his home? Or did you first inform the personage to whom the child psychiatrist would later refer as 'the biological mother'? In the choice of a mother biology clearly wasn't cutting much ice with the child.

For some time she had hinted on the weekly access visits that she'd like to live with Ben and the Mama he had brought her from America.

'They don't like me,' she said of her mother and step-father. 'They whisper to each other.'

Latterly, when it was time for her to be taken home, she had hidden under a bed or in a closet, gingerly feeling along the line that separated pure mischief from getting her point over. On the last two visits tears had got the point over unambiguously enough. Ben and Annie had begun to worry in earnest, but without dreaming of this. She had run nearly two miles in sweater and skirt on a dripping winter's night. A Saturday, just on pub-closing.

'Mama, I had to come home.'

Drops of water ran from her hair and she shivered as her engine wound down.

She had planned her escape and meant it to be more substantial than this, more definitive. It was a kind of seediness she was rejecting, nothing criminal; morning tempers, the four-letter words that spiked the adult sarcasms, a stack of Danish pornography glimpsed in a cupboard left half open, the punctilious appearance at dinner of the nicely chilled Niersteiner yet the failure of clean socks and underwear to arrive in her drawer with comparable regularity until she had learned to wash them herself by hand.

'My panties are always grey,' she said, 'I never get them white when I wash them.'

Well, they wouldn't club her to death with her grey panties, Ben had thought, but they were colouring her view with them.

With her mother's attention on preparations for the evening's lasagna, she had gone upstairs to her room. She liked the room because it was small and hers, except on windy nights when the branches of trees along the back lane would sweep across the big streetlamp. Sinister flickerings and twisted shadow-shapes pushed through the curtains on to her bed. But Gumbo helped. Gumbo didn't wear a cap of Valenciennes or a velvet hood like the dainty doll from France in Daddy's song, but a purple hippo sent from America the day Daddy and Mama got married had its own magic. He went into the duffel bag first, pioneering the packing. Then there were the things you really need to have, especially the school things. Going to school from Daddy's would tell everyone that his house was her every-day, not just her Sunday place. On impulse she retrieved her history book from the bag, scored out the address on the brown wrapper and began to write Daddy's. Kitchen noises warned her that in a minute she would be called to dinner. She replaced the book and put the bag deep in her closet behind a pile of hockey gear.

' "Little barrels roped and tarred," ' she thought, surprised by her memory, ' "Put the brushwood back again, and they'll be gone next day." '

She had no appetite for the lasagna but thought she had better eat something. Mustn't make them suspicious. Pleading a slight headache, she asked for a small helping. After dinner her mother and step-father had arranged themselves in front of the television in the sitting room, she in long dress, eye-shadow and platforms, he in polo-neck and flared slacks to give the lie to his paunch and his balding. With Gauloises and Madeira they were the performers, the figures on the screen an unwitting, captive audience. Charlotte's mother and her husband were devotees of the theatre; this was their Saturday act. Sitting in the room with them Charlotte hoped they wouldn't notice how bulky she was made by the heavy red sweater she had put on to be ready for the cold outside.

When the news came on she got up and left the room. They would think she had gone to the bathroom or to get a book. In any case, news time was sacrosanct; her step-father liked to be informed and her mother would not disturb his concentration by moving from the couch on which they both sat, long-stemmed glasses in hand. That gave a good twenty minutes, just long enough. Up in her room the weight of the duffel bag surprised her when she lifted it from the closet and by the time she got it downstairs to the basement the rope was hurting her hand. She set it on the floor and took down her school raincoat from the row of pegs in the narrow passage. With the coat over her arm she heaved up the duffel bag by its rope and found that she was trembling. The back door still had to be opened. She put the bag down again and dumped the coat on top. The big door was sticky with damp and she had to pull on the handle with both hands.

Wind gusted in at her and rain smacked on the water collected in the badly drained area, but it was the wildly flickering lamp in the lane that forced her back into the doorway, like an escaping prisoner dodging a spotlight. She couldn't face the back way. The lane would be muddy and the trees made big pockets of darkness. Maybe she should wait for a better night or make her escape in daytime. Something tilted over inside her as plan yielded to instinct. Leaving the duffel bag and coat where they were, a lumpy blue cairn by the door, she turned and ran lightly along the passage, up the stairs to the ground floor and past the still-closed sitting room door. Movement made her feel better. She opened the front door. As she closed it behind her and caught the rain and wind on her face, she let out a thin, gurgling yelp of jubilation.

At first she was conscious only of her own motion as she ran. The wind was behind her and she flew. Faces ballooned out of the darkness at her and were left behind. She turned into the next street and saw the pub ahead, a gash of red at its door where the wet pavement reflected the neon sign. The same colour as her sweater. The smell of wet wool rose at her from the garment and she thought it was funny how the cold rain turned warm when it touched her. A group of drinkers outside the pub stared at her and a drunk on the other side of the street waved jerkily.

'Aw ma wee darlin' – didyi go an' miss yer bus? Is that no rotten.'

She began to notice the cars, alert for her step-father's white Renault. News time would be over now and she could feel a stitch coming. Daddy's song came into her head and she fell into its rhythm – 'Five and twenty ponies, Trotting through the dark' – but almost stopped when a police car slid past and the driver seemed to peer at her. She slowed to walking pace. But it wasn't wrong, what she was doing. Going home. She picked up speed again.

The last stretch was downhill but the wind was catching her side now and the stitch was worse. She couldn't stop to rest because they'd know she'd gone and would be after her. Her feet hurt when they struck the pavement and the backs of her legs pricked. For a panicking moment she thought she wasn't moving at all, just jumping up and down stupidly on the same spot. She wanted to cry but couldn't do that and run at the same time. She promised herself she would cry later. There wasn't long to wait. Daddy's tenement was at the next corner, red sandstone walls slick in the rain, a glistening fortress.

Lawyer McLaren was home, snug in suburbia, when Ben rang.

'Basically, in law, the child's place is with the mother since she has custody,' he said. 'It would probably be best for the child if her mother would agree to allow her to remain in your house for tonight, but, logically, it would be quite wrong to approve what the child has done or to give her the impression that she can just decide to take up her abode with you. The fact that the child has absconded from her mother's house changes nothing, basically.'

Mr McLaren was much given to logically and basically, twin pillars of conveyancing vocabulary, no doubt, but real question-beggers in the murk of divorce and custody. Ben replaced the receiver, picked it up again and dialled the number of the house from which he and his daughter had both fled.

'You will either return her within half an hour,' said Charlotte's mother, 'or I shall come and fetch her.'

'My lawyer thinks it would be better if you were to let her stay here tonight,' Ben said. 'Let's face it, she's put herself through it. The kid's beat.'

'Very well. You will return Charlotte to me no later than noon tomorrow.'

After a bath and cocoa Ben and Annie got her to bed. She was distressed by her technical failure. It was humiliating to think of her mother and step-father's finding the bag and raincoat abandoned by the back door, proclaiming her, after all, just a child, unequal to the darkness of the lane.

'But anyway,' she said, squeezing Annie's hand, 'they'll know I mean it now. They said they didn't believe me when I told them I wanted to live with you. But now I've run away.'

'Well, parcel,' Ben said, 'we'll need to have a chat and see what's best.' How's that, Mr McLaren, he thought, non-committal enough for the law?

'Daddy, can we do "Five and twenty ponies"? It's ages since we did it.'

Sunday morning was still wet with a high wind. They all slept in, and when breakfast was over it was time to take Charlotte back to her mother's. She was pale, clearly apprehensive, but there were no tears. In an old Burberry of Annie's with the sleeves turned up she looked comic enough to deflect pathos. She hugged Annie, said she loved her, and turned to Ben with the business-like air of one who wished to get on with the matter. She held his arm on the bus but without clinging, and spoke only once to say again that they would have to believe her now.

'Well, Charlotte,' her mother said, 'I'm very distressed by what you have done. And I know Daddy is too.'

Ben and Charlotte stood facing her in the front hall. Two errant children taking their row. Charlotte reached for Ben's hand but, under the baleful eye, dropped her arm to her side and looked at the floor.

'Oh, yes. I'm distressed too,' Ben said, 'but I think Charlotte's trying to tell us something.'

'Oh, do you indeed?'

'Yes, well, I mean, it was a rotten night,' Ben said. 'She must have felt pretty desperate to go out in it like that.' Dear God, how paltry. Where were the ringing tones of all the fantasy encounters? Silenced by the firm of McLaren, logically and basically.

'I am very sorry that Charlotte felt she wanted to do what she did last night. This is her home and she must settle down in it. I hope we shall have no more of this nonsense, Charlotte.'

'But I told you I wanted to live with Daddy,' Charlotte said, 'And you wouldn't believe me. You're supposed to want me to be happy so you should let me. Don't you want me to be happy?' Her mother had once accused her of being a bad actress but the question was splendid.

'I think you should go now,' her mother said, looking straight at Ben, left eyebrow raised. Ben stepped back towards the door.

'No, Daddy, no!' the child screamed as she ran at her father. As Ben's arms took her he wondered irrelevantly what the step-father was doing with his afternoon. Charlotte's mother grabbed her shoulders and pulled. For a second the child spun free, then was back in Ben's arms, clamping her body to him.

'Take me with you, take me with you. I can't stay here. Take me with you.'

'Charlotte, parcel. Listen.' Ben felt his stomach clench. 'We're all going to talk about it, what's happened, and we're really going to make the arrangements that will be best.'

Spent now, she said nothing. As her grip relaxed Ben gently detached himself from her arms, opened the front door and went quickly out to meet the weather she had run through a few hours before.

'Christ,' he said. 'Christ. Jesus Christ.'

Walking away, he lifted his head to take the rain on his face. He began to run, praying for a stitch in his side as the song his daughter loved came to him in mocking double time. The wind snatched trash from the gutter and scattered it. A swirl of newspapers climbed the wind, showing white against a rain-darkened tenement.

Laces for the lady.

The Drowning

Alan Seymour

The best thing about Shirley and Alan was their casualness. They accepted his mystery, the mystery of blank, stammering, dithering Mr Murdoch, even seemed to think it funny that someone could just 'pop up' as they put it in their strange city. Mr Murdoch was not even clear how or where he had met Shirley and Alan but he wasn't clear about anything.

For some months that year it was, for Mr Murdoch, touch and go. (He knew he was Mr Murdoch because that was the name in his passport.) He'd had what people still called a 'breakdown'. When he woke up and looked about, blinking and puzzled, he found he was in Beirut, which was not so improbable as he had been living, though in quite another country, not far away. Dimly he remembered squalls of temperament, storms of emotion, sullen silences, then a final, bitter combat, verbal, a hasty packing, a flight on the first available plane. Somehow he'd found, or someone had found for him, a small, half-furnished apartment in the Hamra district (how beautiful the raffish, hard-living town was then, before the self-destruction) and looked out across the roofs of white apartment buildings to a haze of blue-purple mountains, and the Mediterranean's blue.

First he must have slept a lot. Now, a small amount of money left in travellers' cheques and cash, he wandered, exploring the place. ˈ

Someone must have introduced him – perhaps in that cramped, pseudo-Austrian bar with the phoney pinewood decor – to Shirley and Alan. He liked them because, though it was clear that they felt a certain obligation to keep an eye on him, they made no fuss. A loose rein. It was on one of his days out alone that he encountered Brucie and Dave.

The names gave him a clue to himself. Growing up in that distant country he'd always found irritating his family's habit of abbreviating two-syllable names. In his childhood there were no Davids, only Daves. More exasperating still, they lengthened short ones. Now, how many years later, in a Beirut street, he heard a grown man calling his mate – naturally not his friend but his mate – not Bruce but Brucie.

Late in the afternoons he would go sometimes to a film. One warm day, at about five, he took a bus from the Hamra district (a little like the Cross, said Shirley, a Sydney girl) and enjoyed the run along the lower main street and the brown-stone wall of the American University – which had groomed most of the Middle East's prominent anti-Americans of recent decades.

The bus began the descent to the old city, along narrow streets tall-sided with apartments, to an odd, diagonally opening corner with one of his favourite, because unexpected, places. A pet-shop, it splashed the colours of South American macaws through its plate-glass windows. As the bus passed it and he decided, early even for the early session, to get out and walk back and look at the birds again, he noticed a flash of bare thigh, bare leg, bare feet on the pavement below. Surely not a girl, bare-legged in shorts, in this still orthodox place? He glanced back through the dusty bus window. Odd sight in an Arab city, two young men in crutch-length shorts, as brief as bathing costumes. Open shirts, very short sleeves, showed the familiar sun-warmed skin of these parts. One of the young men wore thong sandals, one was, strangely in the world of Arab decorum, walking barefoot. Non-conformist young, even among the Moslems? The bus moved on.

At the next stop he stepped down from the bus, walked slowly back towards the exotic pet-shop. The two young men in shorts had discovered it and were talking, joking loudly, with a parrot on a tall perch on the pavement outside. They were not Arabs. They were certainly not Arabs. The voices startled him, all too familiar but strange in this context, unexpected, not heard for years. Would he speak or walk by? Why speak? Why make connections with a kind of people now remote from him and remembered with a certain discomfort? He passed, looked into the window of the next shop but without seeing anything, turned and moved back.

'What part are you from?' he heard himself asking, quietly. 'Sydney? Melbourne – ?'

'Jesus!' One of the boys almost snarled it. 'Why does every bastard think there's only two places in the whole of bloody Australia?' Then, the voice edged with aggression under a conciliatory smile, 'Why? You been there?' One day, the thought darted by, he would write a book about his countrymen and call it *A Chip on the Shoulder*.

'I'm from there.' He half grinned, felt foolish, sorry he'd started this.

The one with the red-brown hair smiled. He had a red-brown beard too, short, combed, neat. And a quietness. The other, the almost straw-coloured blond, turquoise-eyed and with a creamy-toffee tan, absolutely as typical as a travel poster, was the noisy one. This Kodachrome man now thrust out a hand, hugely gripped his own in a grip which almost pulled him off his feet and announced, 'I'm Dave. This is Bruce. Hey, Brucie, another one. The bastards are everywhere.' And before Brucie could speak, confided to Mr Murdoch, 'Every bloody where. Paris, London, Rome, Teheran, Kabul, Katmandu, Karachi, you name it. Worse than bloody Americans now.'

(Oh, the list of cities. Those were the golden days when one could still get about that world.)

They told him their story. They were co-drivers (their own expression) of a Minibus Marathon overland journey from London to Singapore. Bruce, the quiet one, was on the tour for the first time, on their way through to England, Dave a veteran of five trips.

'You were right, anyway,' Dave conceded. 'I'm from Sydney, he's from Melbourne.'

'There you are then,' he started to say, but Dave glared at him, suspecting satire, and he added, 'What's it like, a long trip like that?'

'Be all right if it wasn't for the passengers.' Dave's dialogue was generously sprinkled with four-letter words which Mr Murdoch, to his own surprise, found he mentally – even as they were uttered – edited out. 'Ten of them. All right if you get a good crowd, but Jesus they can be a bloody nuisance. Not bad, this trip. Bit of cunt.' This time the word had come, so loud and unexpected, that the editing process missed it. 'They start out like Sunday school teachers, wouldn't say "shit" for sixpence, you don't let that fool you, they'll all be in it.'

Bruce laughed and Mr Murdoch detected a faint embarrassment. 'He's talked like that the whole trip.' And turned to Dave. 'Not all, mate, don't exaggerate.'

'I've seen cunt in about fifty fucking cities. And it's all the same, all ends up the same.' He started to elaborate, detailed some of his experiences in Bombay, Baghdad, in European cities, in Sydney. He rolled his eyes, boosted his prowess, a grotesque, asserting a virility which nobody had questioned. Mr Murdoch, only a few years ahead of these two, felt a hundred years old. Dave was now doing obscene jiggy-jig motions. A middle-aged Beiruti couple, passing, looked at him, a little startled, moved on. Bruce was laughing again, quietly.

Mr Murdoch was sorry he had stopped, sorry he had spoken, sorry he had ever got off the bus to look at the damned macaws he saw almost every day and didn't intend to buy anyway. Dave ramrodded on, loud in judgement, of women, of Europe ('finished, had it'), of Asia ('Jesus, the stink'), of the poor food outside his home country ('can't get a decent steak anywhere'), of beer or the lack of it. Bruce nodded sometimes, occasionally edged a word in, 'Wasn't as bad as that, Dave.' It was too symmetrical, Dave the Sydney larrikin playing it to the hilt, Bruce the soft-spoken Melbourne gent, they were stereotypes he had never believed in. He wanted them to say something fresh, to prove themselves individuals. They were cartoon people. They couldn't be true. They were.

And as for Arabs . . .

This for a moment sparked a genuine interest in Mr Murdoch. Their present route he had not travelled but knew something of the countries just east of Europe, and liked to be in them, to feel ancient, hard buildings and landscapes about him. These two had seen all those hidden wondrous countries. He wanted to discover them too. Beirut, much as he liked its dazzles of energy, the sense of congestion, crime, sex and money all around, Beirut was too glib, too bent on modernity. A hankering for older places and old races was in him, for old old peoples whose baked cities and villages surely suggested layer on layer of their suffering, their centuries, their knowledge, the deep, ravelled knowledge no young countries could ever have. He knew he was romantic about this, his own local knowledge of nearby places told him so. The reality would be dustier, grimier, stiff with poverty and old empires, at once harder and softer than in any imagining of his. But he desired to partake of that age, to breathe in the dust of a long past, to fill the deeply disliked emptiness in himself and those like him.

'Arabs!' Dave's lips flicked out little blobs of spittle. 'I'd crucify the lot of them. Dirty, smelly, thieving, ignorant, cheating lot of bastards. At the Iraqi border the other day one pushy shit tried to ride me, some crap about extra visas, visas, I've been through ten times, five each way, they can't tell me anything about visas, big, thick-lipped, oily, smelly bastard, never taken a shower in his life, if you put a bathroom in his house he'd probably use it to shit in.' Dave drew back his arm, fist bunched to illustrate. 'I nearly stretched him.'

That, Bruce's expression suggested, would have caused more trouble than the trivial incident was worth. Dave bludgeoned on. 'Primitive? Slums, you never seen such – dirty? Worst part of the trip, through those places. Complete waste of time. Now, Europe, they got some beautiful places, I give 'em that, very modern. We stayed in a couple of terrific hotels. But this part of the world. Nothing to see, nothing to do. Sand, dust, filthy ignorant people. They've got nothing, they've never had nothing, they never will have nothing.' He ended with one decisive word. 'Uncivilized.'

Mr Murdoch's mental projector flicked quick glittering images, the Blue Mosque of Isfahan, tombs and minarets in Shiraz, columned Persepolis, the great arch of Ctesiphon, opulent baths built for the labouring populations at a time when Europe's kings bathed only in perfume and, it was said, piddled on the marble staircases . . . what about that, he wanted to ask, wanted to shout, what about all that?

(And afterwards marvelled at his ability to visualize the Blue Mosque, minarets, the great arch, and knew they were images, merely, of photographs in coffee-table books, born of no real experience.)

Somehow Mr Murdoch maintained an equable, smiling silence. His body ached, he wanted to get away.

Bruce was murmuring, 'Well, we go through in a hurry. If we had more time to look around. . . .'

Mr Murdoch almost wanted to drag Bruce away, to sit him at a café table, to say, Explain, explain him, explain this Dave to me, I think I have never understood. Mostly he wanted to get away.

'Look around?' Dave echoed. 'I'm patching up tyres with Wrigleys Spearmint, bossing old maids in and out of hotels, fighting managers, trying to stick to timetables, time, what time – ?' And repeated, the fight in him ebbing, there was nothing to see.

To make conversation, to plug the gap, he asked how long they would stay here. Just tonight, leaving at sun-up in the morning. The customers, said Dave, could look after themselves tonight, he and Brucie were looking for a bit of fun. For the first time Dave ran his gaze over Mr Murdoch, really seeing him, appraising him for possibilities.

'How long you been here? Seem to know the place. Any suggestions?' And before Mr Murdoch could paper over that gap convincingly, 'What you got in mind for tonight?'

'I'm going to meet some friends,' he lied. 'Promised.'

Brucie, he noticed, looked disappointed. Had he hoped for some quiet conversation, a relief from Dave's endless patter for awhile? Dave was lean but tall, the whole frame in almost mechanically perfect proportion, his tanned bare feet placed confidently on the sidewalk here as anywhere. Brucie, more physically solid, looked every inch the old-reliable, his few movements neat, unforced, economical. Dave yammered on about the great town this was supposed to be but he'd never found much, except once, but instead of launching into another lubricious anecdote, just grinned and hurried on, 'Where does a bloke go for a woman?' It was good to meet someone who knew the place. . . . His gaze started to accuse Mr Murdoch of treason, of failing to honour his obligations to a compatriot. Stomach closing up, he heard himself half-promising to meet them later.

'Where do you live, hotel, apartment?'

'Apartment.' He added another lie. 'Somebody else's. Staying with friends.'

'Australian? Like to meet them.'

'She is. He's a Scot.'

'We could have a few beers. Ay, Brucie, to get out of pubs and hotels into a decent place, you know what I mean, somebody's home, for a change.'

Stomach ever tightening, he visualized being alone with them. In a long agony of pre-vision he saw Dave drunk, picking a fight because Mr Murdoch was not a good example, not a good example of the species, beating him up. Bruce would try to restrain him but nothing would restrain Dave once all that volatile, free-floating aggression found a focus. And the focus would be Mr Murdoch. A nervous tremble began in him, his buried memories of long-ago bad times, there, stirred and turned in their sleep. He could see in Dave's eyes now a curiosity, a dislike, a certain contempt. He did not know why. Instantly, in the moment of not knowing, knew. He was a criticism of Dave. His whole withdrawn manner, his reserve, his caution, his silence, his lack of jumping extravert enthusiasm, all implied a judgement. Quickly he lied that Shirley was expecting guests in for dinner. Important guests, diplomats, to do with Alan's job. 'Couldn't just lob on them . . .'

Dave either didn't believe him or dismissed diplomats and Alan's job and the dinner party as pretentious devices to evade and deny him.

'I'll try to get away early. You know Uncle Sam's on that corner, where all the university kids go?'

Dave looked about to burst into a diatribe against university kids.

Mr Murdoch added, 'Either there or if it's too crowded the little Arab place next door. You can get a drink there. Look out for me about nine thirty.'

Again he sensed that Bruce had a genuine interest in talking to him and that Dave, suddenly even loud, bullying Dave, might be vulnerable, after all, might quieten and talk and listen sensibly.

But in Bruce's eyes was the suspicion that he was slipping out and would never show up. He invented other details about the Arab place, despising himself, to add conviction, and finally got away.

As he hurried towards the narrow alleys and side streets through which he could escape to a distant downtown cinema, he wondered if they were on together, remembered a girl he once knew (where did she come from? just, as Shirley and Alan would say, popped up), Norma, wasn't it, with the whiskey-sour voice, Norma Porter, joking about the extremely tough, butch-looking crocodile hunters up in the Territory who'd turned out to be 'the campest things since Shirley Temple'. Dave talked too much of his insatiable need of women. Bruce's shyness, half-smile, half-reproof, looked to contain another knowledge. Forget it. Two straight-forward young guys, innocent, open, exactly what they seemed to be, nothing more.

He saw a mediocre film, stayed in the same area to eat as it was halfway across the city from Uncle Sam's, took a bus back to the small apartment down its dark side street. In its one room he stood in darkness, looking out across the rooftops to where the sea must be, then down to the brighter-lit streets, fought a lingering curiosity and desire to talk to them again. Maybe they could help him. Maybe they could straighten out certain ambiguities he felt in himself. Maybe they could tell him who and what he was.

Mr Murdoch went to bed, slept, exhausted, and never did see Dave and Brucie again. But, soon, would remember them.

A few days later Shirley suggested that she take him for a drive out of town ('in our brand-new, second-hand Volkswagen') along the coast and into the hills.

After lunch, as they left the town, Shirley seemed to realize that it was one of his quiet days, drove without gossiping.

When they were well out of town the VW turned off to the right, away from the coast, and took a long, slow hill. They came out on a panoramic point at the edge of a mountain, the coast road ribboning by below, sun-haze drumming so hard on the afternoon sea that all blue was trounced out of it and the water colourless, pale. He felt cheated. The Mediterranean should be blue. He considered that a moment and seconded the motion. The Mediterranean should always be blue.

Just behind them rose a colossal white statue of the Virgin Mary (surely not of stone but of plaster, it looked like a giant garden gnome) and only later did he appreciate the strangeness of that in an Arab country, even one so finely balanced (then) between Moslem and Christian populations. (Later, Alan punned, 'Monumental tactlessness. Christians are never so happy as when they're putting up symbols to impress the heathen of foreign parts.') Other visitors walked about it, read the French inscription celebrating the fate of some sailors of that sea so blankly gazed upon her by her huge white face.

They walked down steps to a cliff-hanging restaurant nearby, drank coffee. Strong black Arab coffee tended to give him the trots, he had noticed, but risked it, needing to be adrenalined into talking again.

'Five times,' he heard himself say, out of a silence.

She had been looking out at the sea-haze, turned to him. A big girl, a little heavy-looking at first but then you noticed her movements were good, competent, graceful, and her face, always without make-up, nice skin, very slightly, lightly, freckled, was a good face, the front for a quick imagination, maybe limited but honest. Don't patronize, he told himself. We're all limited. And not always honest.

'Five times he's done that trip backwards and forwards.' They'd discussed his meeting in the street and she realized immediately what he was talking about, smiled.

'And hasn't seen it. Looked, but hasn't seen.' Now she laughed. He wondered why her laugh, and hers alone, did not make him instantly irritable. 'But that's our problem,' she was saying. 'We make too much of all that, some of us, once we get abroad.'

He guessed what she meant. Beirut Airport. Couples poring over maps, guidebooks, brochures. Swapping suggestions over coffee. 'It says Ba'albeck is a must.' 'Too far.' 'Only two hours, it says here.' 'Gertrude, not another ruin.' 'Alec, if we've come all this way.' Determined Australian women. Why didn't they hand the country over to them? Seemed more masculine than the men.

David and Brucie still hung in his head, on trial. Even quiet Brucie could not be let off. No guts. By his muted smiling acquiescence he had endorsed Dave's arrogant ignorance, and this was worse, for he looked to have the intelligence to challenge it.

If he could think without aching, it would help. 'What will happen?' he heard himself ask.

'To you?' She smiled again, shrugged. These shrugs meant a policy of non-involvement. Why blame her? He had appeared from nowhere, undergone his ordeal of breakdown and partial amnesia, if that's what it was, she was helping him through, gently and, though kindly, at arm's length.

'You don't know. I don't know.'

Shirley lifted her coffee cup to sip, didn't sip, looked out at
the sea through the dusty window. 'Superb view so they don't
clean the windows. Odd.'

A fly crawled across the table. Did all restaurants have this
kind of plastic-topped table now?

'Is this Formica?' he asked.

She looked down at it. 'Something like it.' Glanced up
suddenly at his face, his eyes. 'You remember the damnedest
things.'

He wished the other people, few though they were, would
go away. He could fall to his knees, bend his head to her lap,
ask her to stroke his hair while he wept. Or sucked his thumb.

'Why not – don't be offended – a psychiatrist?' He shook his
head. 'An ordinary doctor, then?'

'No. Not yet.'

'You know what you need,' she began, tentatively, as
though it had been on her mind and the moment was judged to
be the right one. 'To forget yourself and your own problems
for a bit and put all your energies into something else.'

Mr Murdoch agreed, not knowing, of course, how soon
he'd be given the opportunity.

They went back a different way, following a narrow road
along the ridge, with shops and little mountain houses on each
side. A small booth flowered into colour with its piled fruit
and vegetables. Shirley stopped the car. 'They're cheaper up
here. And so fresh. That's the theory anyway.' He liked this
tiny, high-hanging village. Across the road was a small white
stand, a kind of freezer, outside a pastry shop. They bought
locally-made ice cream. One was green, from pistachio nuts.
They ate it by the roadside and got back into the car, laughing,
fingers sticky.

'This,' she announced, taking a different road back down
the sharp slope to the coast, 'is supposed to be breath-taking.
Take a breath.'

Bends, a ravine suddenly giddying away at his side (yet no
impulse to open the car door, to step out into space, to try to

fly, which he half expected of himself at first glimpse of the mighty drop to the coastal plain) and always the vast dazzled span of sea thrown back into the eyes at every turn.

At the side of the road ahead a car was parked. A man stood beside it, pissing, facing in towards the road. Shirley started to giggle. 'Took some getting used to. They all do it. Anywhere. Against the nearest wall. Vacant lots. No false modesty. Never turn their backs.'

'Exhibitionist!' He yelled the word at the man who didn't understand it. Again he and Shirley were laughing. He'd begun to relax.

They were nearing the level road beside the coast. He looked back at the mountain behind them. From the city it looked purple, or almost, with a permanent thin haze of salt and dust. From here it looked rich and green with umbrella pines, oaks and plane trees. He enjoyed thinking about the modulation of its colours, his mind taking a rest from himself. A sudden flutter of white, high against mountain-top and sky. Oh, white Christian arrogance. The statue of the Madonna.

As they moved fast along the beach road, back towards town, they noticed, well ahead, a few cars drawn up at one point, on their side, the right side, the beach side, of the road. A bare stretch, no buildings screening the sea from them, the beach about sixty feet deep. Close to the road, parallel to it, a train line. Beyond that the yellow-grey sand and the sea. A small bus, old, its paint fading, was pulling up. People started to jump from it, to hop across the trench between road and rail-track, then to stream, dozens of them, across the narrow beach. From other cars, now stopping, other people leapt and ran.

Shirley was slowing down. 'A film, maybe. They make a lot of films here lately. Exotic Beirut. Spies. Gun-runners. Drugs. We often see them on location.'

She stopped the car. They looked to the small crowd gathering near the water's edge. It was not a film unit. His heart began to stammer at him. Watch from here? Get out for a closer look? No involvement. At the same second they opened their doors.

A swimmer was being carried in from the churned-up, white shallows. They saw him lugged by a couple of youths in swimsuits, his wet heaviness slippery in their hands, his head lolling drunkenly, body almost slipping back into the water. They clutched more desperately at him, got him ashore. The crowd gathered around, pressed in.

Mr Murdoch tried to let out certain orders, ideas, instructions, a specific knowledge, all hammering at the inside of his head. Shirley cried out, 'Give him air, give him air.' Nobody understood her language. They kept crowding in, not to help but to shout suggestions, to comment, to gossip in the high buzzing enjoyably scandalized Middle Eastern fashion. She hung back. He waited beside her. A muddled comment mumbled out of him. 'We're supposed to know what to do.'

Trying to push through the small crowd ringing the man, they moved forward. As people dodged this way and that they glimpsed him, stretched on his back on the sand. Wet, gleaming. Sand dry-patched parts of his body. He wore an old-fashioned, white-belted, crimson bathing costume. A thick-set ugly man, about forty, forty-five. Bald in the centre. Black hair wet and untidy, profuse, out of balance with the bareness at the centre. The mouth was open, gasping, he thought for one second, then decided it was quite still.

But there was something wrong. His brain was trying to spin instructions to Mr Murdoch. Something drastically, vitally incorrect about what was being done.

'Shouldn't he – ?'

'Not on his back,' Shirley was saying to someone. She tried to mime; turn him over. Nobody took any notice. Again she did it, both hands reversing positions in mid-air. And mouthed it, in case anyone understood. 'Over.' The man stayed as he was, on his back, on the sand.

Vomit oozed from his mouth. A white foam of sea water and bubbles, like the shallows he had been carried from. Or had they swum out to him? Had one of the adolescent boys, now buzzing about importantly, pretending to know what to do, the pretence barely covering a fine panic, had they seen him from the beach, swum out to him? How far? What had he been doing there, swimming alone, at this unpopulated part of the beach, only a couple of kids nearby? An accident? An attempt at suicide?

People were shouting and pointing back at the road. A taxi had been waved down and was now pulling in. They pointed at it. The driver stepped out and immediately got into argument with another man. A fat little woman in a cheap, print skirt joined in, abusing the driver. Insisting.

The two youths and an older man grabbed at the man who had almost drowned (or had he drowned? was he gone already? difficult to tell with that ooze at his mouth) and began to carry him up the beach towards the taxi. The driver was shouting and his hands went wild, with the charged, dramatic, God-strike-me-dead-if-I-am-not-an-honest-man gesticulations he enjoyed in the locals. But as he and Shirley moved with the crowd, following or keeping beside the carried man, Mr Murdoch kept gasping with the attempt to say whatever was trying to be said. 'The wrong way,' he got out at last. 'They're carrying him the wrong way.'

Each of the boys had grabbed a leg, near the ankle. The man helping them had managed a grip below the shoulders, hands hooked into the armpits. The victim was being carried, face up, head lolling, more slop oozing from his mouth. It looked wrong.

Shirley cried, 'Face down, he ought to be face down . . .' Then a sudden doubt. 'Oughtn't he?' And turned to Mr Murdoch. 'How do they do it back home?'

'Can't remember. It looks – can't we do something?' Suddenly he was almost screaming. 'It looks all wrong.'

A hundred images of a thousand days, a beach childhood, long surf, the whitest sand, exercises, men, teenage boys, always doing exercises, with a reel. And club members getting out there, fast, powerful, always efficient, getting the lifeline to the victim, but only exercises, a practice, a kind of game, attaching the lifeline to him, getting him back. So what did you do when there was no club member, no reel, no lifeline?

He and Shirley were staring at each other, mouths open, hopelessly, each struggling with the same imperfect memories and their own idiot paralysis.

'We've got to do something.'

'How?' she yelled, the first and only time he ever heard her raise her voice.

'They'll kill him.'

If he isn't already dead.

Some were yelling in Arabic, some in French, and, seeing them, strangers, excited, upset, wanting to help, even in snatches of English. 'Hospital' he kept hearing, or a word close to it. They were lifting the oozing man across the railway track and now the small ditch to the taxi. The taxi driver looked important, anxious, and sorry he had ever pulled up.

'But how far is it to the hospital? Will he make it?'

There was one on this side of town, she thought. Words he had been trying to release from his mind suddenly broke free. Holger-Nielsen. Resuscitation.

On the beach, in gymnasium at school, they'd learned the technique, practised it. Hands pressed to each side of the lungs, a gentle pumping. Something like that.

And then a solution came to him and he felt an abrupt and blissful pride. Of course he knew the answer.

Kiss of life.

Mr Murdoch ran around to the other side of the taxi. Now the crowd was bigger, hysterical or sounding it, all screaming at once, arguments flying up, where to take him perhaps, what best to do. The driver was in his seat, another man, middle-aged, modestly dressed in a worn suit and open shirt, was getting in beside him. The youths and half a dozen others were bundling the victim in his crimson swimsuit into the back seat of the car and one of them, two of them, my God, three of them, were trying to climb in after him until an older man dragged them out, all but the first one who looked alone, frightened, responsible. The swimmer was still on his back, on the seat. Hadn't any of them heard of artificial respiration, of even the most elementary things to do? But had he known, remembered, jumped in and taken over, organized, done anything useful at all?

'The window,' he shouted. Nobody heard or noticed. He pointed to it. Tried it – the word appearing miraculously in his mind as he needed it – in French. Banged his fist against it. Yelled again. For God's sake at least open the window and let the man breathe in some air if he could. If he could breathe at all.

But that was it. The answer. Kiss of life. Of life of life of life.

'Looks bad.' Shirley's voice came flat and quiet beside him. 'Doubt he'll get there.'

'Kiss of life!' he shouted at her. 'Couldn't I – ?' He was trying to wrench open the rear door on the passenger's side. It was locked. Guiltily, he was thankful it was locked.

'Do you know how to do it?' Shirley, rightly, looked doubtful.

'No!' He was shouting still. 'I could try. Worth a try.'

The man's head had fallen back and hung below seat level over the floor. 'Get his head up,' he yelled. 'Up.' Nobody took any notice.

Seeing him struggling still, the boy in the car leaned across the up-ended body, pressed a button. The rear door swung open.

Well, there you are. It's open. Nothing between you and the victim.

He spoke not to her now but to himself. Ought to try. At least ought to try. They've buggered this man's chances, done everything wrong, at least give him one more go at it.

But that old, dread, Anglo-Saxon reluctance crept over him. Reluctant to draw attention to himself. To do anything too odd, too unexpected, too – and how silly it sounded in the dramatic circumstances – too dramatic. Nonsense.

He leaned forward into the car. The eyes of the rescued man stared straight into his. People were shouting, arguing, moving, all around the car. The eyes, startling against his black hair, were blue. And his skin above the crimson trunks had none of the beautiful pale brown of most local complexions but was white, dead white. The eyes fixed him. Mr Murdoch couldn't move, leaned forward stiffly into the car, looking at the blue eyes looking into his own blue eyes and wondering, Are they dead? Are those eyes dead already? Or just glazing, unconscious?

Kiss him, he ordered himself. The taxi was about to leave, the driver yelling back at a dozen urgers at each side, roaring the accelerator. Kiss him, he repeated. Get in there, go with them to the hospital, breathe into that man on the way, You don't know how, learn as you do it, it can't be so difficult, give him a chance, even if it fails let him have a chance.

The eyes stared at him. No expression, no accusation.

He couldn't. His stomach was compressing and decompressing at the thought, at the horror. Ashamed, in anger, he thought the awful impulsive irresistible thoughts he would be a long time forgetting. I can't. The dead eyes. The dead flesh. The dark-red lips, dead. The disgusting slime of white vomit caking at the mouth and down the chin, slithering down cheek and throat. I can't. Can't put my mouth to that mouth, to that filth.

He pulled back. Someone else slammed the door, the taxi was already in gear and moved away. Everyone stood looking after it, quietening now. Tears, of shame, burned his eyes. He turned away from her, tried to blink them then to wipe them away. They got back into the Volkswagen.

The rationalizing began immediately. As soon as the VW started to move off they both found reasons. A perfect stranger. Looked dead and gone already. (But that he would never know, of that he would never be certain.) We're foreigners here. Wouldn't be thanked for interfering. If anything went wrong. If the man did die before reaching hospital, if he were already dead, no matter how accidental the cause, they might be only too pleased, only too pleased, to have a foreigner to blame. For meddling, for sucking the breath out of him, covering his mouth, impeding his breathing. They would find a dozen reasons why this kiss of life should never have been applied.

And the final, sweetest, rationalization of all. Who were they to interfere? How did they know he didn't want to die? Had he been calmly on his way to a desired, solitary death when the youths found and rescued him? Perhaps it would have been more of a crime to bring him back to that life he was desperate to leave? Who would ever know?

'But how helpless can you get?' Shirley asked. 'We grew up with all that. I lived not three hundred yards from the beach. Saw that sort of thing all my life.'

'I know, I know.' Even as they talked the images obediently presented themselves for his inspection. The tall upright figures with the small, tightly-fitting caps, carrying the body face-down, not quite horizontal, head tilting forward slightly, the whole organized movement so neat, so impeccable, not a joint out of place. Those superbly proportioned young men, lifesavers, what a beautiful, now he thought of it, beautiful, apt, extraordinary, unique word. Lifesavers, knowing exactly what to do and doing it, repeatedly, at beach after beach, saving over so many years so many lives. Now he could see every movement, yes, *now* he could, the whole, concise, economical, pragmatic, romantic, *life*-saving technique (was the man in the taxi dead yet?) rhythmically unrolling, a perfect ritual. Nobody in this sludge of a place seemed to have heard of . . . wait a moment. Hardly fair. Not a regular swimming beach, no guards on duty, nobody around. In any case, dare he accuse anyone? Now he could see and recall with perfect clarity, or at least well enough to be able to reproduce them if asked, all the movements, movement by movement, that would have contributed to keeping the rescued man alive a little longer, given him his chance. Now he remembered, when the panic was over, when memory was of no use.

After a while, deliberately, to massage their self-bruised sensibilities, they talked of other things, tried to joke a little.

Later, at their apartment, over a whisky, Alan said, 'You did exactly the right thing.'

'We did nothing. What right thing?'

'Kept out of it.'

Alan had lived here for years, was absorbingly interested in the local politics but not, Mr Murdoch thought, in the people as people. He detailed all the grisly possibilities had they involved themselves. The hospital authorities would have been suspicious, first. Then the police, when they were called in. Who were you? Why had you interfered? What was that you were trying to do? Hadn't your negligence helped to kill the man? (But was he dead? Perhaps at this moment he was smiling weakly from his hospital bed at a kind nurse, at the youth who'd helped.) And by what right did you interfere with a purely local problem?

Alan told them a story.

'When I was in Bombay years ago . . .' Alan, a very white-skinned, very hard-thinking gritty kind of man who treated everything and everyone with impartial scepticism, was not the most immediately likeable person. But any toughness he had was no doubt, thought Mr Murdoch, hard-won over years of jostling with strange people in strange places.

'I was in a hired car on my way to the airport. About to leave. A busy street. The clutter, the mess of humanity, all that. A kid ran out from nowhere, right in front of us. Driver braked but no chance. I felt the wheels ride over the body. The driver's eyes – poor terrified little rat – his eyes got very white in his dark brown face. I could see them in the rear-vision mirror looking to me. I shouted, "Drive on. Don't stop. Drive straight on." He did. We just vanished in those jam-packed streets. If anyone took his number the police could deal with him later. After I'd gone. I got to that airport and took the plane and got out of there.'

He wanted to say, couldn't even begin, 'Wasn't that a bit?'

In any case Alan could read the embarrassed, careful set of his face, and answered the unspoken comment.

'Nothing else to do. India. You know India. You don't know India? The police. The mess. The bureaucracy. As a foreigner there I wouldn't have stood a chance. Looking for a scapegoat. Fix it on the foreigner. It was an accident. The driver was not speeding, not unduly. The kid came from nowhere. Nobody's fault. Certainly not mine. I was leaving. . .'

It went on a bit too long, he felt, Alan protesting too much, even now, so much later, uncomfortable about it. (As they would be about their drowning?)

'Anyway, my company wouldn't have been too happy at having me hang around there for days, weeks, might have been months by the time the law, Indian law . . .' And then, the story wrapped up quickly, the conclusion drawn. 'No, you did the right thing. Didn't get involved.'

Shirley looked about to demur but didn't. Mr Murdoch needed to argue, but restrained himself. A certain hard glitter in Alan's eyes suggested just how happy he'd have been had this unbalanced stranger been fool enough to involve his, Alan's, wife in such an incident. They changed the subject.

But he was glad of the Indian story. As the chat went on and he sometimes took part, sometimes listened, he was coming to a decision. They had helped enough. Their casual companionship had seen him through. It was time to move on, and to sort out his own problems in his own way.

The drowning was not forgotten so easily. In bed that night, seeing it all again, alone and admitting his guilt, he heard the phrases he had buried today dinning again in his head. Dead flesh, dead lips, disgusting, oozing mouth. And ugly. The face was so ugly. Put lips to that? If it had been a beautiful or even a nice-looking or even a plain woman. If it had been even a good-looking or at least a better-looking, healthier-looking man, one whose unfortunate ugliness and oozing death were not so repellent. . . This was the new criterion? Only the pretty shall live. In the darkness now he admitted his shame, to himself at least. Faced the awful triviality of his emotions at that profound, death-facing moment in the taxi.

He was definitely not a good example of the race. On the beach he had felt today a helplessness that was absolute.

And then, just before he slept, a thought, simple and deadly, slipped into his mind.

Dave and Brucie would have known what to do.

Notes on the Authors

Anne Aylor was born in New Mexico and has lived in London for eight years. Her work has appeared in *New Stories 5*, *New Poetry 7*, *London Magazine* and *Stand*. In 1980 she was a runner-up in the BBC Radio 3 short story competition with the final chapter of her recently completed novel, *Pictures in a Darkened Room*.

Julian Barnes was born in Leicester in 1946. His first novel, *Metroland*, won the Somerset Maugham Award. His second novel, *Before She Met Me*, has just been published by Cape.

A. R. Barton is English and lives in Zürich. Previous publications include a story in *New Stories 6*.

Colin Beadon was born in Maymyo, Burma, in 1935. His father was a colonial police officer, and his mother died before he knew her. He came to Trinidad in 1949 where his father was posted as a police chief. He went to sea when he was seventeen for three years. After two years in British West Indian Airways, Trinidad, as a mechanic trainee, he joined the oilfields in 1957 as a 'roughneck'. He worked his way up to rig superintendent, which took him to Venezuela and St Lucia. He is now working again in Trinidad and searching for a geothermal contract anywhere along the San Adrian fault.

Alison Brackenbury was born in 1953. Her first collection of poems (*Dreams of Power*: Carcanet New Press, 1981) was a Poetry Book Society Recommendation.

John Haylock, educated at Aldenham School, in France and at Pembroke College, Cambridge, served as a liaison officer with the Greek Army. After the war he taught in Baghdad and wrote with Desmond Stewart *New Babylon: A Portrait of Iraq*. His first novel, *See You Again*, was set in Japan; his second, *It's All Your Fault*, in Thailand and Laos. *A Different Party*, a novella, has a Moroccan setting. He contributed regularly to *Blackwood's Magazine* and writes for *London Magazine*, which, in June 1980, published *One Hot Summer in Kyoto*. He is now teaching English literature in Tokyo.

Glyn Hughes's books include *Best of Neighbours* (Selected Poems), Ceolfrith Press, Sunderland, 1979; a prose book about Yorkshire, *Millstone Grit* (Gollancz, 1975, and Futura paperback) and one on Greece, *Fair Prospects* (Gollancz, 1976). He published his first novel, about eighteenth-century Yorkshire, *Where I Used to Play On The Green*, with Gollancz early this year. The story included here is one of a series which he is still writing, and which link together imaginatively treated episodes from a childhood spent in Cheshire. For the past eighteen years he has lived in West Yorkshire.

Morris Lurie was born in Melbourne, Australia, in 1938, to which city he returned in 1973, following seven years abroad. He has published four novels, four collections of stories, three collections of reportage, two books for children, and a volume of plays. His stories have appeared in the USA in *The New Yorker*, *Antaeus* and *The Virginia Quarterly Review*, in England in the *Sunday Telegraph Magazine* and *Punch*, and in many other leading magazines; been widely translated and anthologized, and broadcast on the BBC. Morris Lurie is married, and has two children.

Nancy Oliver has had a radio play broadcast by the BBC and short stories published in a number of periodicals including the *London Magazine*. After working as a full-time journalist, she now edits a magazine which appears twice yearly. She has read economics and philosophy at two English universities.

Peter Parker was born in Herefordshire in 1954, and was educated in the Malverns, Dorset and London. He appeared on the Fringe at the 1977 and 1978 Edinburgh Festivals as actor, writer and director. He has since worked as a char and as a bookseller. In 1979 he was awarded second prize for a short story in the Wandsworth All-London Literary Competition. He is a regular contributor to *Gay News*, and lives in South London.

Patrick Riordan was born in the North of England in 1948. He studied painting at Winchester School of Art from 1968 to 1971. He started writing in 1971, in Winchester, where he lived at intervals until 1975. He now lives in Boscastle, Cornwall, and works full-time as a handyman at a hotel in nearby Tintagel. He is married with two young children.

John Rudge was born in 1945 in Birmingham, and read English at Cambridge before going into publishing. He lived in West Africa for a year and later travelled in Scandinavia as a publisher's representative. Since 1971 he has lived in Amsterdam, where he works as a freelance translator.

Alan Seymour, Australian-born playwright, novelist and television writer, has lived in London since the 1960s when his then controversial play *The One Day of the Year* was staged here after its original Australian tour. His novel *The Coming Self-Destruction of the United States of America* was published in 1969. During the 1960s and 1970s, apart from theatre criticism for the *London Magazine* and *Plays and Players*, he worked mainly in television, adapting stories by Jean Rhys, the L. P. Hartley trilogy *Eustace and Hilda* and (in 1981) Antonia White's *Frost in May* novels. Now he is completing a stage play and a film for Channel 4.

Anne Spillard was born in Leeds, and is now living in Cumbria. Her stories and poems have been published and her work broadcast on Radio 4 and Radio Lancashire. She has taught many subjects at many schools over a period of fifteen years. She has a daughter and a son.

Graham Swift was born in London in 1949. His short stories have appeared in various magazines and anthologies including *New Stories 3* and *5*, and work of his has been broadcast on BBC Radio. He has published two novels, *The Sweet Shop Owner* and *Shuttlecock*, both with Allen Lane. *Shuttlecock* appears this year as a Penguin paperback. *Learning to Swim*, a volume of his short stories, also appears this year from London Magazine Editions.

James Thurlby has always been involved in writing, first in journalism, then in communications in industry. Now he devotes himself full-time to the writing of fiction, an activity that other responsibilities for many years made sporadic. He has had a number of short stories published and works with critical compulsiveness on a mulch of facts and fancies that appear in some danger of acquiring the characteristics of a novel. A Yorkshireman, he has a degree in philosophy from Trinity College, Dublin.

Marshall Walker was born in Glasgow in 1937 to a Scottish actress and an English accountant. He studied and taught literature at Glasgow University, with spots of time in Africa and the USA. Married, with five emphatic daughters, one muddled cat, and a red wheelbarrow, he lives for the present in Hamilton, New Zealand, where he is Professor of English at Waikato University. He has written critical articles, short fiction, and *Robert Penn Warren, a Vision Earned* (1979). It takes him about four years to write a short story, and he does not admit to working on a novel.